World Wisdom
The Library of Perennial Philosophy

The Library of Perennial Philosophy is dedicated to the exposition of the timeless Truth underlying the diverse religions. This Truth, often referred to as the *Sophia Perennis*—or Perennial Wisdom—finds its expression in the revealed Scriptures as well as the writings of the great sages and the artistic creations of the traditional worlds.

The Gospel of the Redman appears as one of our selections in the Spiritual Classics series.

Spiritual Classics Series

This series includes seminal, but often neglected, works of unique spiritual insight from leading religious authors of both the East and West. Ranging from books composed in ancient India to forgotten jewels of our time, these important classics feature new introductions which place them in the perennialist context.

The Gospel of the Redman

Commemorative Edition

Compiled by

ERNEST THOMPSON SETON

and

JULIA M. SETON

Foreword by PAUL GOBLE

Introduction by DEE SETON BARBER

World Wisdom

Collected from the Old Indians
during fifty years of friendly
intercourse

by Ernest Thompson Seton

&

6ᵃ May - 1945
Julia M Seton

All the line drawings inside this book are the work of
Ernest Thompson Seton

Ernest Thompson Seton and his wife Julia M. Seton

The Gospel of the Redman
Commemorative Edition
©2005 World Wisdom, Inc.

Most recent printing indicated by the last digit below:
10 9 8 7 6 5 4 3

Library of Congress Cataloging-in-Publication Data

The gospel of the Redman / compiled by Ernest Thompson Seton
and Julia M. Seton ; foreword by Paul Goble ;
introduction by Dee Seton Barber.–
Commemorative ed.
p. cm. – (The library of perennial philosophy.
Spiritual classics series)
Previous ed. entered under E.T. Seton.
"All the line drawings inside this book are the work of Ernest
Thompson Seton and his wife Julia M. Seton."
Includes bibliographical references and index.
ISBN 0-941532-76-3 (pbk. : alk. paper)
1. Indians of North America–Religion. 2. Indian mythology–North
America. I. Seton, Ernest Thompson, 1860-1946. II. Seton, Julia
M. (Julia Moss), b. 1889. III. Seton, Ernest Thompson, 1860-1946.
Gospel of the Redman. IV. Series.
E98.R3G67 2005
299.7–dc22
2004029644

Printed on acid-free paper in the United States of America.

For information address World Wisdom, Inc.
P.O. Box 2682, Bloomington, Indiana 47402-2682
www.worldwisdom.com

CONTENTS

FOREWORD

Surely the darkest years for Native Americans were the three generations from 1877, which marked the end of the wars and the start of confinement on reservations, until 1972 and the occupation of Wounded Knee by the American Indian Movement, which helped Indian people find renewed confidence in themselves, and started a renaissance of the culture generally.

During those early dark years there were few voices raised in support. There were anthropologists and ethnologists traveling the reservations to publish obscure museum and society pamphlets, valuable in themselves, but having a limited readership. Ernest Thompson Seton was a light shining during those dark years. There were others: Frank B. Linderman, Thomas B. Marquis, George Bird Grinnell, Hartley Burr Alexander, Melvin R. Gilmore, James Willard Schultz, and in later years, Grey Owl's fine books. All of these gave first-hand knowledge of Indian peoples, but nobody spoke to such a broad audience as Seton. Although he was published in both New York and London, his books were more popular in England and Canada than in the United States, where Native Americans and the natural world were either taken for granted, or too close for comfort.

Seton was born in South Shields in the north of England, 1860. The family came upon hard times and emigrated to Toronto, Canada when Seton was six years old. He later studied art in London and as a lifelong student of the natural world in Canada, he became Naturalist to the Government of Manitoba. He founded the Boy Scouts of America and the Woodcraft League.

He was a superb storyteller, and he had that wonderful and rare ability to speak about his specialty, primarily the natural world, in language which could be understood by both children and adults, and he also had the ability to sketch and paint, and to illustrate his stories. He published, in New York and London, *The Biography of a Grizzly* (1899), *Wild Animals I Have Known* (1901), *Lives of the Hunted* (1901), *Monarch the Big Bear* (1905), *Animal Heroes* (1905), *The Biography of a Silver Fox* (1909), *The Trail of the Sandhill Stag* (1914), and many more.

Seton knew Indian people, and it was his books, *Two Little Savages* (1903) and *Rolf in the Woods* (1911) which stirred the imagination of those interested in Native Americans. If you want anthropological or ethnological information, you do not turn to Seton. More important, he sensed, and knew how to communicate, the Native American spirit.

On a personal level, and I am sure I speak for many people, Seton's *Two Little Savages* was a great influence in my life. The book was a favorite of my mother and I know I asked her to read it more than once before I learned how to read. I am sure, like many others too, I grew up wanting to be like Yan in the book, who was, I learned later, based much upon Seton's own younger days. The book was the spark which lighted my lifelong love of the world of Nature and all things Native American.

When I came from London to live in the Black Hills, I was forty-four years old. Among the few things I was able to bring with me from England were my old much-loved Ernest Thompson Seton books, and here they are still, loose pages, bindings falling apart, yet to be treasured, I hope, by another generation. It is an honor, therefore, to write these few words to Seton's, *The Gospel of the Redman.* May the book never go out of print because its message is changeless. And, may it also open up the treasure-trove of Seton's other wonderful books!

PAUL GOBLE
June 2004

E.T. Seton

E. T. Seton
at age 22½ — Art Students' League
1883

Self-portrait, 1883

PREFACES TO THE 1937 AND 1948 EDITIONS

PREFACE TO THE 1937 EDITION

In March, 1905, we were in Los Angeles on a lecture tour. The morning after the lecture, we were met at the Van Nuys Hotel by some Eastern friends who, addressing the Chief,[1] said: "We have a message for you. There is a strange woman in the Hills who wishes to see you." Accordingly, we took the tram to the end of the track, then set out on foot to climb what, I think, are now called the Beverly Hills. On the green slope higher up was a small white cottage; in front of this, a woman dressed like a farmer's wife. She waved her apron as we approached.

She was introduced to us as a Mahatma from India, although born in Iowa. She had left her home as a small child, had spent many years studying under the Great Masters, and was now back on a mission to America. She was a strange looking person. We could not tell whether she was thirty or a hundred and thirty years old. Her skin was like yellow parchment, and covered with thousands of faint lines not deep enough to be wrinkles. Her eyes had the faraway veiled look of a mystic. Her talk was commonplace as she served coffee and cakes. We wondered why she had sent the summons.

Finally, after an hour, we rose to leave.

---

[1] Ernest Thompson Seton was known the world over as "The Chief," a title bestowed originally when he headed the Boy Scouts of America.

Then, suddenly, she turned on the Chief with a total change of look and demeanor. Her eyes blazed as she said, in tones of authority: "Don't you know who you are?"

We were all shocked into silence as she continued: "You are a Red Indian Chief, reincarnated to give the message of the Redman to the White race, so much in need of it. Why don't you get busy? Why don't you set about your job?"

The Chief was moved like one conscience-stricken. He talked not at all on the road back, and the incident was not mentioned for long after. But I know that the strange woman had focused his thoughts on the mission he had been vaguely working on for some years. He never during his long life ceased to concentrate on what she had termed "his job."

Therefore, after years of research, we have deemed it our duty and our privilege to compile the results of our labors into a concrete message.

* * *

When the manuscript was complete we were visited by a Jewish rabbi, a profound scholar, who, after a careful reading, said: "But this is straight Judaism!" We were glad of his endorsement. Some weeks later, two Presbyterian ministers from the Eastern States declared that "it was exactly what the modern Presbyterian Church taught."

A Greek Catholic Archbishop assured us that it was "pure Catholicism, divested of certain rites and ceremonies."

A Quaker said it was just what his Church preached; and a Unitarian minister declared it "the purest Emersonian Unitarianism." Finally, a Mason said it was nothing but the teachings of his Order.

So it would seem that it must be real religion since it is universal, basic and fundamental. As a corollary, then, it must be acceptable to a world seeking a way out of dogma into truth.

* * *

In compiling these records of Indian thought and culture, we have been assisted by a committee of men and women whose lives have been given to such studies. Some are Indians; some, White folk. Without their approval, nothing has been included in this book.

The Indians are:

CHIEF STANDING BEAR, Sioux, author of several books on Sioux life.

SUNFLOWER, Sioux, colleague of Standing Bear, lecturer.

WALKING EAGLE, Ojibway, lecturer, student of Indian life.

OHIYESA (Dr. Charles A. Eastman), Sioux, lecturer, author of books on his own people.

ATALOA, Chickashaw, lecturer, author, former head of Art Department of Bacone College.

JOHN J. MATHEWS, Osage, author, lecturer, graduate of Oxford.

CHIEF OSKENONTON, Iroquois, lecturer, singer.

The Whites are:

MARY AUSTIN, author of many books on Indians and other subjects.

DR. EDGAR L. HEWETT, archaeologist and author, representing the School of American Research, etc.

KENNETH M. CHAPMAN, author, lecturer, representing the Laboratory of Anthropology.

DR. GEORGE BIRD GRINNELL, author, lecturer, life-long student of Indian life.

JAMES MOONEY, author, representing the Smithsonian Institution.

DR. F. W. HODGE, author, lecturer, representing the Southwest Museum.

MRS. LAURA ADAMS ARMER, author, lecturer, member of the Navaho Tribe by adoption.

JULIA M. SETON
On board the Queen Mary
January 22, 1935

PREFACE TO THE 1948 EDITION

Since the last edition of this little book, the Chief has passed on to even greater achievement than was his in this world. But he speaks through these pages with the same sincerity of purpose which dictated the several earlier issues.

Although known best as a writer of animal stories, he dedicated a large part of his life to helping the Indian wherever he could; but more, to helping the Whiteman realize the value of the doctrines by which the Redman lived in the days of his unspoiled grandeur.

Born out of time, as are all great men, he foresaw the need of the world today, and it is with the hope of spreading what he called the Gospel of Manhood that we offer this new edition in love and lasting reverence for the ideals for which he stood.

JULIA M. SETON
Los Angeles, California
January 11, 1948

INTRODUCTION

Ernest Thompson Seton, the "Black Wolf," was an award-winning wildlife illustrator and naturalist who was also a spellbinding storyteller and lecturer, a best-selling author of animal stories, an expert on Native American sign language and an early supporter of the political, cultural and spiritual rights of First Peoples. He was born August 14, 1860, in South Shields, Durham, England, of Scottish ancestry (both sides of the family fought for The Old and New "Pretenders" and therefore had to leave Scotland after 1715 and 1745). Seton's name at birth was Ernest Seton Thompson, which he later changed as an adult. He was the eighth of ten brothers that lived—one sister died at age six. Due to several business failures, the Thompson family, with the exception of a couple of the older brothers, immigrated to Stony Creek, Ontario, four miles outside the town of Lindsey where they would become farmers. There were very few people living near or around the Thompsons in their new surroundings; they were "pioneers" in the most fundamental sense of the word, and it is in this that a clear foreshadowing of attitudes that Seton held central to his philosophy of "back to the earth" later in life can be found. Even at a very early age, Seton's interest in and love for nature and the world outside the walls of his home were remarkable. One of the only ways that his mother was able to get him to sit still as a toddler for more than a minute was to tell him, "You are a tree. Trees do not move," and thus he would sit motionless for more than an hour. When Ernest was slightly older, he began to show the beginnings of a concern for nature that would indicate the extraordinary man he would eventually become: he and his cousin were chasing chickens around the yard one day with fishing irons, and after they caught one, they skewered it but they did not eat it. Although entertained at the time, a forlorn Ernest was said to be later filled with feelings of remorse and revulsion at his "bloodthirsty, savage acts." He was five years old at the time.

Seton's father, Joseph, made a poor farmer, so by 1870 they moved to Toronto where he was employed as an accountant. Young Seton attended Toronto schools for his basic education. His 1903 book, *Two Little Savages*, later recorded his youthful adventures in Toronto's ravines. As a young man, Seton became interested in art and in 1876, at the age of 16, he produced his first oil painting "The Sharpshin Hawk." Seton created 4,000 paintings, drawings and sketches during his lifetime. A woman prominent in the Toronto art community became his mentor in this field, giving him advice and money to continue his studies. He won the Gold Medal for Art before he was 18. At the age of 19, he went back to England to apply for a scholarship at the Royal Academy of Art. He won, through a juried entry, a seven year scholarship that he did not complete. Because he was under age, according to the rules of the British Museum, he sought and was granted permission, for life, to use the resources of the library by the then Regents— the Prince of Wales and the Archbishop of Canterbury.

By 1881 his health (from poor food and living conditions) was so bad that a cousin wrote his mother saying that she had better get him back to Canada before he died. His family sent him a steerage ticket and he went back to Toronto. Two of the older brothers were homesteading in Manitoba, near what is now the small town of Carberry. In 1881 he went by train to join his brothers where he spent many of his formative years. These were "the golden years, the best days of my life," wrote Seton of the Sandhills and Spruce Woods of Carberry. These landscapes and his first contact with the Native Peoples of North America influenced Seton to write *Trail of the Sandhill Stag* which was published in 1889. His natural history mentor was Dr. William Brodie of Toronto who had a son close to Seton's age. They had done natural history studies in Toronto before and after the English expedition. In 1881, Seton published his first article, "Key to Birds of Canada."

Seton made a worse farmer than his father. Always distracted by natural surroundings, this was the time of his most active animal art and research. He counted every feather on the wing of a grackle by candlelight. He would go off into the Carberry Sandhills for days and weeks on end and was thought to be lazy and odd by the conventional people of the town. Here he wrote his first natural history articles and began exchanges of study skins with other naturalists both in Canada and the United States, including Theodore Roosevelt.

His first visit to the United States was in December of 1883. He went to New York where he met with many naturalists, ornithologists and writers. From then until the late 1880s he spent his time between Carberry, Toronto and New York. He became an established wildlife artist, and was given a contract in 1885, by the Century Company to do 1000 mammal drawings for the Century Dictionary. He did many of those drawings at the American Museum of Natural History, and became life-long friends with Frank Chapman, William Hornaday, Coues, Elliot, and many others. He also spent some time at the New York Art Student's League where his bronze sculpture of "The American Bison" was highly praised. In 1884, he returned to Europe and studied art in Paris, France. This was where he did the research for his first book, *Studies in Art: The Anatomy of Animals*, published in England. While speaking with his publisher in England, he met the author Mark Twain for the first time. Seton's painting "The Sleeping Wolf" hung in the Paris Salon in 1891.

In 1892, Seton was appointed Provincial Naturalist, Government of Manitoba, Canada, an office he held for the rest of his life. His books, *Birds of Manitoba* and *Animals of Manitoba*, are still respected references to this day. Due to the heavy eye strain caused by the close work on the *Anatomy* book, Seton was told that unless he did not use his eyes heavily for at least six months he would be blind. So he left France and went to the ranch of a man named Fitz-Randolph where they hunted for the Lobo, the famous marauding wolf in the New Mexico Territory. He was sorry to kill such a fine animal, but he did not destroy "Lobo's" spirit—Seton adopted the wolf paw print as part of his signature. The story of "Lobo" was first published in Scribner's Magazine and then with other stories in book form as *Wild Animals I Have Known*. From then on Seton's fame as a writer spread throughout the rest of North America and into Europe. This book has never been out of print, and has been published in a dozen languages. Rudyard Kipling wrote to Seton that the idea for the Jungle Books came from *Wild Animals I Have Known*. A stream of other books of animal stories soon followed, including *Biography of a Grizzly* (1900), *Lives of the Hunted* (1901) and *Two Little Savages* (1903). His reputation as a naturalist, author, illustrator and storyteller spread rapidly all over the world. But some controversy ensued—John Burroughs, a prominent naturalist, attacked Seton in the Atlantic for ascribing self- consciousness, motives and emotions to animals. He later accepted the evidence of Seton's scrupulous field observations and became a friend and colleague. Burroughs later wrote, "Seton easily throws all other animal story writers in the shade." Seton wrote approximately 10,000 scientific and popular articles during his lifetime. He received an honorary Master's Degree in Humanities from Springfield College, MA.

In spite of Seton's intensive writing, he still managed to find time to paint as demonstrated in his work, "Triumph of the Wolves," which was exhibited at the First World Fair in Chicago in 1893, as the entry from Manitoba. Originally "Triumph" was first painted and exhibited in Paris, France in 1891. This painting created considerable controversy because it portrays the reality of the natural world from the wolves' perspective. Seton married for the first time in 1896, to Grace Gallatin, a wealthy socialite, who was also a pioneer traveler, founder of a women's writers club, a first rank suffragette, and a leading fund-raiser for War Bonds in WW I. She died in 1959. Their only child, Ann, was born in 1904 and died in 1990. Ann, who wrote under the pen-name of Anya Seton, composed historical novels that were very popular. Several were made into movies in the '40s and '50s. In 1900, the Setons moved to "Windygoul" Cos Cob, Connecticut. Seton expanded his conservation work. He was later celebrated as a seminal non-Native environmentalist by the Native Americans. Seton gave 6,000 lectures in North America and Europe during his lifetime. His message, based substantially on the wisdom of the Native Elders, has proven to be singularly prophetic.

In 1902, Seton wrote a series of articles for Ladies Home Journal which would inspire him to create an organization that would change lives forever—the Woodcraft Indians. More than anything else, Seton believed firmly in "youth, adventure, the great outdoors and the idea of physical fitness based on sports and rigorous exercise to revitalize the American character." Seton thought that the solution to the deterioration of

America was to be found in America's young people. In his opinion, industrial growth and the expansion of urban America were causing the country and its youth to lose many of the positive attributes which had enabled them to become so great in the beginning. He said that "money grubbing, machine politics, degrading sports, cigarettes, town life of the worst kind, false ideals, moral laxity, and lessening church power, in a word, 'city rot' has worked evil in this nation." Seton wanted to change all that and when the chance came quite suddenly he grabbed it.

Seton had decided to fence part of his property in Windygoul, New York, despite the fact that it had once been a favorite hunting ground of local boys; but after a number of the boys ran rampant on his land, defacing his buildings and killing his animals, he responded in a most unusual way. Instead of seeking revenge, Seton invited the boys up to his house during their Easter vacation to camp out. When the forty-two of them arrived on Good Friday, 1902, for a camping adventure which they viewed rather suspiciously, they were met with an experience unlike anything they had anticipated. Rather than being vindictive towards his young vandals, Seton took advantage of the opportunity their presence afforded him to induct them into his tribe of Woodcraft Indians. For the boys, the vacation seemed rich in ceremony and tradition, for Seton had carefully thought out all aspects of Woodcraft before they arrived. Central to their experience was a main "council ring" where the group spent most of their time. This is where the boys listened to stories of the Plains and Indian life, told by Seton, who would later relate how they "gaug[ed] my stories in a steady crescendo till I had renewed the Fenimore Cooper glamour of romance, and heightened it to a blaze of glory." It is clear that it was quite an inspiring affair for the boys which transcended their previous relationship with their natural surroundings, teaching them a new reverence for natural beauty and nature's creatures. Each boy, as part of the process of "think[ing] Indian" was instructed in the identification of various plants and animals, as well as in the arts of stalking and trail making, and a variety of other Indian games and rituals. As well, each boy had to earn an Indian name, a unique honor, that was given to one boy per camp per year. When the holiday was over, some of the boys were reluctant to leave, for the man whom they had once hated because he had fenced in one of their favorite places to hunt had shown them a previously unknown side of the natural world to which they now felt very strong ties. Many came to idolize Seton as "Black Wolf," his Indian name given to him by the Lakota, and some even viewed him as a father figure.

The appeal and success of Seton's holiday retreat spread rapidly, and, due to his active promotion of Woodcraft throughout the region, camps with different leadership, but following the same set of noble ideals, sprung up all over the Northeast. Seeing the rising popularity of his following among the young men of America, Seton decided to write a handbook for Woodcraft use, to clear away ambiguities about tradition and ceremony, and thus he published *The Birchbark Rolls of the Woodcraft Indians* in 1903. Twenty-eight editions were published until 1930. One of the essential features of Woodcraft is that it requires judicious updating to incorporate new ideas and realities, without losing its essential features. More and more boys became "braves" in the first decade of the twentieth century, and by 1910, it was estimated that more than 200,000 were either alumni or currently involved in what had become a prominent movement in the restoration of America's understanding of its Native American past. Woodcraft, as it came to be known, was the forerunner of the Boy Scout movement, and a major influence on the Girl Guides, Cub Scouts, the YMCA and the Canadian and American Camping Associations.

Seton's influential book was given to Lord Robert Baden-Powell in England in 1906. The two later met at the Savoy Hotel in London to help develop the Boy Scouts organization. Seton was chairman of the founding committee of Boy Scouts of America in 1910. He served as Chief Scout from 1910 until 1915. However, Seton did not like the military aspects of Scouting, and Scouting did not like the Native American emphasis of Seton. With WW I approaching, the militarists won, and Seton resigned from the Boy Scouts. In 1912, the Woodcraft League of Czechoslovakia was founded. As well, in 1916, the Order of Woodcraft Chivalry was founded by Ernest Westlake in England and over the years was started in Belgium, France, Canada, Poland, Germany, Hungary, USSR, Ireland and Yugoslavia.

Seton revived Woodcraft in 1915, not as a children's organization, but as a co-educational organization serving all ages, called the Woodcraft League of America. Seton was universally called Chief in connection with Woodcraft. The Black Wolf name was conferred on him by the Sioux, whose language (one of several) he spoke. He preferred this name to his own. Board members of the Woodcraft League of America included naturalists John Burroughs and Frank Chapman, businessmen David Abercrombie, John Alexander and James E. Sullivan, plus James L. Hughes (Inspector of Public Schools, Toronto, Canada), Edgar Robinson (Secretary of the International YMCA), Charles D. Walcott (Secretary of the Smithsonian Institute) and Ambassador Henry Van Dyke of Princeton University. President Theodore Roosevelt was Patron and coined "Blue Sky," the traditional greeting of Woodcrafters everywhere. Roosevelt defined Woodcraft as "a man making scheme with a blue sky background." Seton wrote, "Woodcraft is something to do with what you have." The first "Totem Board"—an occasional news-bulletin of Woodcraft news, activities and ideas—was published in 1917. A year later, Seton published *Sign Talk*, a study of Native linguistics, the result of 20 years periodic travel and research among many Native Nations in the western United States and Canada. In 1921, he also helped establish a program for children aged 6-11 called "brownies" which later became the basis for the Girl Scout Brownies. The Woodcraft League prospered. In 1922 the children's organization "Little Lodge" was merged with the Western Rangers, and became the Woodcraft Rangers. They were not interested in girls or adults, so this became a young boy's organization. The Woodcraft Rangers became a co-educational organization by the early 1950s.

Between 1918 and 1925, Seton researched and wrote the major four-volume scientific work, *The Lives of Game Animals*, which solidified his reputation as a biologist. The volumes contained 1,500 illustrations. He received the "Silver Buffalo Award" from the Boy Scouts of America, the first year it was awarded. Seton went to study and live with the Sioux and Pueblo Indian Peoples in co-operation with Clyde Fisher, Head of the Hayden Planetarium, American Museum of Natural History, in 1927. It was here that Seton wrote *The Gospel of the Redman* which demonstrates his lifelong appreciation and advocacy for the culture and traditions of the First Peoples. Seton was later awarded the internationally prestigious "John Burroughs Medal" by the National Institute of Sciences in recognition of *The Lives of Game Animals* in 1928. In 1920, he also received the "Daniel Giraud Elliot Medal" by the National Academy of Sciences for "pre-eminence in zoology." He also played a key role in founding the American Cub Scouts, which borrowed liberally from Woodcraft. Seton continued to run the

Woodcraft Leadership Camps from his Greenwich, Connecticut home until 1930 when he moved to Santa Fe. In 1930, at the age of 70, he became a United States citizen.

In Santa Fe, he built a castle on 2500 acres in his "retirement" and continued to train leaders in Woodcraft. In addition to this, he wrote most of the first U.S. edition of the Boy Scout Handbook and was responsible for many of the concepts found within Scouting throughout the world. Seton also designed and founded the "Seton Institute," a training camp for leaders of recreational organizations based on the North American Indian traditional way of life. In 1934 Seton and Grace were divorced. The next year Seton married his second wife, Julia Moses Buttree (also known as Julia Moss Buttree) in El Paso, Texas. Julia Seton was a student at Hunter College, New York, and an author who wrote extensively on Native arts, crafts and music (e.g., *American Indian Arts, A Way of Life*). Her first book, *Rhythm of the Redman*, which Seton illustrated, was published before they married. Julia worked as Seton's assistant and they both spoke at joint lectures at schools, clubs, and churches throughout the United States, Canada, France, England and the Czech Republic. In 1938, the couple adopted a daughter, now Dee Seton Barber, who appeared with them on stage during Seton's lifetime. She was the custodian of Seton Castle in Santa Fe, New Mexico until it was sold in 2004 and is an expert advisor to Seton scholars, collectors and Woodcrafters worldwide. In 1938, Seton published *The Buffalo Wind*, a short poetic book which describes the call he heard all his life to give voice to the Redman's way of life. Seton published his autobiography, *Trail of an Artist Naturalist*, in 1940. Until 1941, Seton's Woodcraft Leadership camps continued in Santa Fe, but they were not continued after World War II. His last book, *Santana, the Hero Dog of*

France, was published in 1945. Seton gave his last lecture at the University of New Mexico on August 14, 1946. After Seton's death, Julia continued to write and maintain the Santa Fe estate, and also lectured on her own. Her last tour was sponsored by the Audubon Society in 1967. She suffered a stroke in 1968 and died in 1975 in Santa Fe.

The Gospel of the Redman was originally published in 1935 and was written by Seton while he was living among the Indians. Seton was great friends with such prominent American Indian leaders as Chief Plenty Coups of the Crow, Chief Luther Standing Bear and Charles Eastman of the Sioux. Many of these leaders were closely consulted while Seton wrote *The Gospel of the Redman* and they approved the final manuscript for publication. At that time the word "Redman" was one of the most common expressions to refer to First Peoples. In recent years there is a tendency to think that this expression carries a racial connotation, but to Seton and his American Indian friends this word carried a connotation of admiration and respect. We have therefore preserved the title in its original form to honor the work of Seton and the many native leaders who worked together to present an accurate portrait of this way of life.

After Seton's death in 1946, Julia Seton published the 1948 edition of *The Gospel of the Redman* in a modified form by eliminating the chapter on warfare and adding a new Foreword. Her Foreword is preserved in this commemorative edition of the book. This is the only edition of the book to collect and present most of Seton's drawings of American Indian motifs and a selection of photographs that illustrate Seton's life, his role as the founder of the Boy Scouts of America and his friendship with American Indian leaders.

Much simplified, the message Seton delivered for more than 60 years is that a proper understanding and respect for Nature can provide a type of antidote to many of the difficulties brought on by our modern technological world. And, the spiritual traditions of the First Americans provide us with profound insights into the proper understanding of man's role in the universe. *The Gospel of the Redman* presents Seton's message, and the message of the American Indians, in its essential form.

DEE SETON BARBER
June 2004

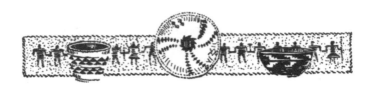

I

THE GOSPEL OF THE REDMAN

There is no Indian Bible written by an Indian, just as there was no Pentateuch written by Moses, no Tripitika by Buddha, no Dialogues by Socrates, no Gospels written by Christ. All these records were made long after by those who knew their Master in his lifetime, or at least received the traditions of his teachings from those who were privileged to hear his voice.

I have never yet had an Indian tell me fully and frankly the details of his faith; but by respectfully questioning the old men, by assembling their traditions, by noting their customs, by observing their lives, by gathering the records of their prophets, by consulting living Whitemen who knew the Indian in primitive days, and especially by conferring with Indians who were educated as Whites after spending their youth in the ancient way of their people, we have achieved something like a comprehension of the Indian's creed, of his unwritten laws, of his sense of relationship and duty to the Great Oversoul, the Creator and Ruler, as well as to his neighbor and to himself.

In a Continent of this size, with hundreds of different Tribes and variants of culture, there are very different details of established thought. Among these, I have selected the highest and best that were native; and, as a whole, adhered to the philosophies of the great Tribes such as the Sioux, the Cheyenne, the Ojibway, the Iroquois, the Shawnees, the Pueblos, the Navahos, the Aztecs, and the Mayans.

Naturally, I have followed the leaders of thought in these Tribes, attaching especial value to the teachings of Wabasha, Kanukuk, Sitting Bull, Crazy Horse, Wovoka, and the magnificent Tecumseh. My watchword is, "The best things of the best Indians" just as we ourselves hope to be represented by our best brains and kindest lives, not by the ruffians and outlaws that form so large a part of our population.

The Indian teachings in the fields of art, handicraft, woodcraft, agriculture, social life, health, and joy, need no argument beyond presentation; they speak for themselves. They are what we need; and in offering them here, I do so realizing that the Redman is the apostle of outdoor life, his example and precept are what the world needs today above any other ethical teaching of which I have knowledge.[1]

But his spiritual message is more important, and less understood.

---

[1] Having seen many Englishmen take to the Indian life, Bacon thus offers unwitting testimony to the naturalness and sanity of the Redman's way: "It hath often been seen that a Christian gentleman, well-born and bred, and gently nurtured, will, of his own free will, quit his high station and luxurious world, to dwell with savages and live their lives, taking part in all their savagery. But never yet hath it been seen that a savage will, of his own free will, give up his savagery, and live the life of a civilized man."

II

THE SOUL OF THE REDMAN

HIS SPIRITUALITY

The culture and civilization of the Whiteman are essentially material; his measure of success is, "How much property have I acquired for myself?" The culture of the Redman is fundamentally spiritual; his measure of success is, "How much service have I rendered to my people?"[1] His mode of life, his thought, his every act are given spiritual significance, approached and colored with complete realization of the spirit world.

    Garrick Mallery, the leading Smithsonian authority of his day, says: "The most surprising fact relating to the North American Indians, which until lately had not been realized, is that they habitually lived in and by religion to a degree comparable with that of the old Israelites under the theocracy. This was sometimes ignored, and sometimes denied in terms, by many of the early missionaries and explorers. The aboriginal religion was not their [the missionaries'] religion, and therefore was not recognized to have an existence or was pronounced to be satanic."[2]

---

[1] Pablo Abeita of Isleta reiterates this in all his public talks on the subject.

[2] "Picture Writing of the American Indians," *10th Ann. Rep. Bur. Eth.*, 1893, p. 461

"Religion was the real life of the tribes, permeating all their activities and institutions."[3]

John James, after living sixty years among the Choctaw Indians of Texas, writes: "I claim for the North American Indian the purest religion, and the loftiest conceptions of the Great Creator, of any non-Christian religion that has ever been known to this old world....

"The North American Indian has no priests, no idols, no sacrifices, but went direct to the Great Spirit and worshipped Him who was invisible, and seeing Him by faith, adored Him who seeketh such to worship Him in spirit and in truth, who is a Spirit and planted a similar spirit in His creatures, that there might be communion between the two."[4]

In 1834 Captain Bonneville visited the Nez Percés and Flatheads before they had been in contact with Whites, either traders or missionaries, and sums up these wholly primitive Indians: "Simply to call these people religious would convey but a faint idea of the deep hue of piety and devotion which pervades their whole conduct. Their honesty is immaculate, and their purity of purpose and their observance of the rites of their religion are most uniform and remarkable. They are certainly more like a nation of saints than a horde of savages."[5]

Tom Newcomb, my mountain guide in 1912 and 1914, was an old scout of the Miles campaign, who lived with the Sioux under Crazy Horse for some years in the early '70s. He said to me once (and not only said,

---

[3] Picture Writing of the American Indians," *10th Ann, Rep. Bur. Eth.*, 1893, p. 231.

[4] *My Experience with Indians*, 1923, p. 67

[5] Washington Irving, *The Adventures of Captain Bonneville*, 1837, p. 171. Father de Smet came many years later—i.e. 1840—and began his mission in 1841. He was the first of the missionaries; but obviously could claim no credit for this condition.

leather headband

feather strip on quill

red cloth wrapping

Brow-bands

Finished feather

E.T. Seton

but dictated for record): "I tell you I never saw more kindness or real Christianity anywhere. The poor, the sick, the aged, the widows and the orphans were always looked after first. Whenever we moved camp, someone took care that the widows' lodges were moved first and set up first. After every hunt, a good-sized chunk of meat was dropped at each door where it was most needed. I was treated like a brother; and I tell you I have never seen any community of church people that was as really truly Christians as that band of Indians."

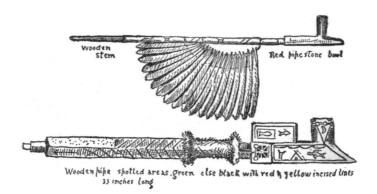

Wooden stem   Red pipestone bowl

Wooden pipe spotted areas, green else black with red & yellow incised lines
33 inches long

RELIGION

The idea of one Great Oversoul is widely spread among the Indians; not universal, perhaps, but much more widely spread than in the Old World.

All of our best Indians believe apparently in one Great God. From among many recorded statements, I quote the following by Grinnell. In his discussion of the Pawnee belief in the Great Spirit, whom they call Tirawa, he says: "Tirawa is an intangible spirit, omnipotent and beneficent. He pervades the universe, and is a

Supreme Ruler. Upon His will depends everything that happens. He can bring good or bad; can give success or failure. Everything rests with Him...nothing is undertaken without a prayer to the Father for assistance.

"When the pipe is lighted, the first whiffs are blown to the Deity. When food is eaten, a small portion is placed on the ground [or in the fire] as a sacrifice to Him."[6]

Other Tribes, each in its own tongue, acknowledge the one Great Spirit. Orenda, Manito, Wakonda, Olelbis, Agriskoue, Maona, Tirawa, Awonawilona, etc., are among the names by which He is worshipped, sometimes as a personal God, sometimes as an impersonal all-pervading Spirit; but with a completeness of worship that has valuable lessons for other peoples and races.

Some superficial observers maintain that the Indians were Sun-worshippers. To this, Ohiyesa, the cultured Sioux, replies: "The Indian no more worshipped the sun than the Christian adores the Cross."[7]

Catlin writes of the primitive Indians on the Missouri: "The North American Indians are nowhere idolaters—they appeal at once to the Great Spirit, and know of no mediator, either personal or symbolical."[8]

Their breadth of view and complete toleration are reflected in a saying attributed to Wabasha and Red Jacket: "If any man do anything, sincerely believing that thereby he is worshipping the Great Spirit, he *is* worshipping the Great Spirit, and his worship must be treated with respect, so long as he is not trespassing on the rights of others."

---

[6] George Bird Grinnell, "Pawnee Mythology," *Journal of American Folklore*, vol. vi, p. 113.

[7] *The Soul of the Indian*, 1911, p. 13.

[8] George Catlin, *Manners, Customs, and Conditions of the North American Indians*, vol. ii, p. 233.

Again, by the same prophets: "Trouble no man about his religion—respect him in his view of the Great Spirit, and demand of him that he respect yours. Treat with respect such things as he holds sacred. Do not force your religion on anyone."

THE INDIAN SUNDAY

The Redman's religion is not a matter of certain days and set observances, but is a part of his every thought and his daily life.

Many years ago in Montana, I heard a missionary severely rebuke an Indian for driving his team on Sunday.

The Indian looked puzzled, as he was merely minding his business and caring for his family. The missionary reiterated that this was the Lord's Day. At last a light dawned on the Indian. He glanced up with a gleam in his eye and answered, "Oh, I see. Your God comes only one day a week; my God is with me every day and all the time."[9]

Later I heard the same missionary denouncing an Indian dance, although it was beautiful, clean, athletic, and manly—much akin to the dance with which Miriam celebrated the defeat of Pharaoh, also the dance that King David did to express his joy when the Ark came back to Israel.

The missionary used violent language, and threatened jail and soldiers if the Indians did not cut off their long hair.

I defended the Indians and pointed out that not only Benjamin Franklin and George Washington wore

---

[9] "The sabbath was made for man, and not man for the sabbath."—Mark 2: 27.

their hair long, but the Lord Jesus Himself did—and finally, that Samson made the ruinous mistake of his life when he allowed them to cut off his long hair.

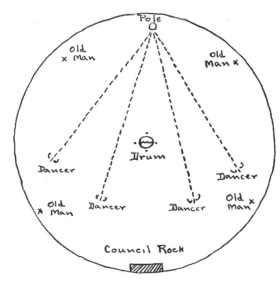

Fig. 65 – Plan of the Sun Dance
of the
Woodcraft Indians

Fig. 66 – Prayer Plume

THE CHIEF AND THE MISSIONARY

A recent book by Long Lance gives some helpful light on Indian thought and worship.[10] The authenticity of the book has been challenged, but the incident here set forth has happened many times, and is incontrovertible in its fundamental truth.

"... The next morning the White minister at the Hudson's Bay Post sent word to the Indians that he was coming over to visit them. The Suksiseoketuk told us that he was going to tell us about the Whiteman's Wakantonka, his Great Spirit.

"When they received this news of the coming of the minister, all of the Indians painted their faces and put on all of their best medicine clothes. The medicine man got out his drum, and soon we were ready to receive him.

"When we saw the minister coming, the medicine man started to beat his tomtom and sing one of his medicine songs; for he thought that would please the visitor who represented the Whiteman's 'medicine' and Great Spirit. Our Chief went out and met the minister and shook his hand, and then took him over to meet our minister, the medicine man.

"After they shook hands, the minister made a speech. He told our medicine man that he was preaching something not worth while. He said: 'I didn't mean for you people to fix up like this; I meant for you to wash the paint off your faces and put your medicine drums away. There is only one God in Heaven, and I am here to tell you about Him.'

"Indians never interrupt anyone when he is talking, even if he should talk all day—that is an ancient courtesy among Indians—so everyone stood and lis-

---

[10] *Buffalo Child Long Lance,* 1928, pp. 148-51.

tened to the minister while he told us of the Whiteman's God. He made a long speech. He said that the Indians must lay down their arms and live peacefully alongside the Whiteman who was coming into his country.

"When the missionary finished his speech, our Chief arose and addressed him. He said: 'Why do you tell us to be good? We Indians are not bad; you White people may be, but we are not. We do not steal, except when our horses have been raided; we do not tell lies; we take care of our old and our poor when they are helpless. We do not need that which you tell us about.'

"'But,' said the missionary, 'there is only one God, and you must worship Him.'

"'Then if that is true,' said our Chief, 'we Indians are worshipping the same God that you are—only in a different way. When the Great Spirit, God, made the world, He gave the Indians one way to worship Him and He gave the Whitemen another way, because we are different people and our lives are different. The Indian should keep to his way and the Whiteman to his, and we should all work with one another for God and not against one another. The Indian does not try to tell you how you should worship God. We like to see you worship Him in your own way, because we know you understand that way.'

"'But the Great Spirit you speak of is not the same one that we worship,' said the missionary.

"'Then there must be two Gods,' said the Chief. 'Your God made a land for you far across the "big water." He gave you houses to live in, good things to eat and fast things to travel in. He gave the Indian the tepees to live in and the buffalo to feed on. But you White people did not like the land that your God gave you, and you came over here to take the Indians' land. If you did that, how do we know, if we should accept your God, that He won't take everything from us, too, when we die and go to your hunting grounds?'

"'But the Indians must learn how to pray,' said the minister.

"'We do pray,' replied our Chief. 'This is the prayer that we pray at our Sun Dance (Thanksgiving): 'Great Spirit, Our Father, help us and teach us in the way of the truth; and keep me and my family and my tribe on our true Father's path, so that we may be in good condition in our minds and in our bodies. Teach all of the little ones in Your way. Make peace on all the world. We thank You for the sun and the good summer weather again; and we hope they will bring good crops of grass for the animals and things to eat for all peoples.'"

THE INDIAN CREED[11]

Through what prophets we know not, but the evidence is beyond challenge that the Redman, before the White-man came, had achieved a knowledge of the Creator of the universe and was worshipping Him in a religion of spirituality, kindness, and truth.[12]

1. THERE IS ONE GREAT SPIRIT, THE CREATOR AND RULER OF ALL THINGS, TO WHOM WE ARE RESPONSIBLE. He is eternal, invisible, omniscient, omnipotent, unportrayable. In and through Him all beings live and move; to

---

[11] There can be no doubt that the following great men, and many more that could be named, held to a creed which was exactly that of the Redman: Abraham, Isaac, Jacob, Joseph, Moses, Aaron, Joshua, Gideon, David, Solomon, Hezekiah, Nehemiah, Jeremiah, Ezekiel, Job, Socrates, Plato, Epictetus, Voltaire, Benjamin Franklin, Emerson, Abraham Lincoln, Walt Whitman, Renan, Ingersoll, and the Masonic Brotherhood, as well as the Quakers and the Jews.

[12] Canon J. S. Bezzant of Liverpool Cathedral, England, said in a recent address at Columbia University, New York: "One should speak of higher and lower religions rather than of true and false religions.

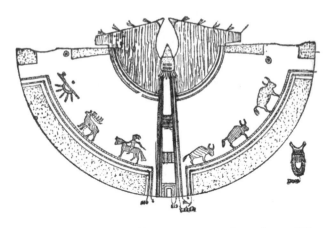

Him all worship and allegiance are due; from Him all good things come. Him we must approach with reverence; His favor may be won by prayer, by sacrifice, and a kindly life; knowledge of Him, by discipline, by fasting, and by lonely vigil; and with that knowledge will come His guidance. He is impersonal; yet at times inspiring or entering personally into animals, birds, clouds, rain, mountains, men or things.[13] Under Him are many lesser spirits.

2. Having arrived on this earth, THE FIRST DUTY OF MAN IS THE ATTAINMENT OF PERFECT MANHOOD, which is the just development of every part and power that go to make a man, and the fullest reasonable enjoyment of

"It is quite impossible to claim that spiritual life, the experiences and insights within one religion, are real; and to declare them entirely false illusions when manifested elsewhere.

"God has not left Himself without witness at any time, and His everlasting power and divinity are manifested in varying degrees throughout the created universe and through the men and women who seek Him."—*New York Herald Tribune*, November 27, 1935.

[13] "This thought in its essence is almost what modern science has attained to—the conception of Nature and God as one."—Dr. E. L. Hewett, *Ancient Life in the American Southwest*, p. 74.

the same. He must achieve manhood in the Body Way, the Mind Way, the Spirit Way, and the Service Way.[14]

3. HAVING ATTAINED TO HIGH MANHOOD, HE MUST CONSECRATE THAT MANHOOD TO THE SERVICE OF HIS PEOPLE. He must, above all, be a good provider for his family, a brave protector, a kind and helpful neighbor, and ever ready to defend his family, his camp, or his Tribe from a foreign foe.

4. THE SOUL OF MAN IS IMMORTAL. Whence it came into this world or whither it goes when it departs, he does not know. But when his time comes to die, he should remember that he is going on to the next world. What the next life contains for him, he has no means of ascertaining. Nevertheless, he should not approach it with fear and trembling, repenting and weeping over such things as he has left undone, or such things as he should not have done. He should rest assured that he has done his best with the gifts and the limitations that were his,[15] and that his condition there will be governed by his record and his behavior here. Therefore, let him sing his Death Song, and go out like a hero going home.[16]

---

[14] Compare Luke 2: 52: "And Jesus increased in wisdom and stature, and in favor with God and man."

[15] There is no tree in the forest that is straight, though all are reaching up for the light, and trying to grow straight.

[16] Every Indian prepared in advance his Death Song. Some of these are given later.

THE TWELVE COMMANDMENTS

1. THERE IS BUT ONE GREAT SPIRIT.[17] He is eternal, omniscient, omnipotent, invisible. He pervades all things at all times. Reverence Him, and respect all worship of Him by others, for none have all the truth, and all who reverently worship have claims on our respect. So also, show respect to such things as are held sacred by others.[18]

2. THOU SHALT NOT MAKE A LIKENESS OF THE GREAT SPIRIT, or portray Him as a visible being.[19]

3. HOLD THY WORD OF HONOR SACRED. Lying is at all times shameful, for the Great Spirit is everywhere all the time. To swear falsely in the name of the Great Spirit is a sin worthy of death.

4. THOU SHALT KEEP THE FEASTS,[20] LEARN THE DANCES, RESPECT THE TABOOS, AND OBSERVE THE CUSTOMS OF YOUR TRIBE, if you would be a good member of the community and profit by its strength. For these things are the wisdom of the Ancients and of your fathers in the long ago.

5. HONOR AND OBEY THY FATHER AND THY MOTHER, and their fathers before them, for age is wisdom; and their

---

[17] There are many lesser spirits, just as certain Aryan creeds proclaim the existence of saints, archangels, angels, ghosts, fairies, goblins, ghouls, and devils. The conception of the Trinity, also the doctrines of Original Sin, of Vicarious Atonement, of Infant Damnation, and of Priestly Mediation, were utterly foreign to all Indian thought and teaching.

[18] When the Indians found that the Cross was an emblem sacred to the Whites, they, according to their custom, treated it with respect, although it meant nothing to them personally.

[19] One may make a likeness of His messenger, the Thunderbird; or His symbol, the Bird-serpent; or of lesser spirits, such as Katchinas; but never of the Great Spirit.

[20] The old Indian Bureau complained that the Indian lost too much time with 30 or 40 of these Sabbaths each year, and proposed to substitute 52 Sabbaths of rest, besides some 20 legal holidays.

discipline of you is surely for your helping and your lasting benefit.

6. THOU SHALT NOT COMMIT MURDER. Killing a member of one's own Tribe, if deliberate, is a crime worthy of death; if by accident, it can be compensated by adequate damages, according to the judgment of the Council.[21]

7. BE CHASTE IN THOUGHT AND DEED, according to the highest standards of your Tribe. Keep your marriage vows, and lead no others into breach of theirs.[22]

8. THOU SHALT NOT STEAL.[23]

9. BE NOT GREEDY OF GREAT RICHES. It is a shame and a sin of all unworthiness in a man to have great possessions, when there be those of his Tribe who are in want. When, by chance of war or of commerce, or the gifts of the Great Spirit that have blessed him with power, he hath more than he hath need of for himself and his family, he should call the people together and give a Potlatch or Feast of Giving, and distribute of his surplus to those that have need, according to their need; especially remembering the widow, the orphan, and the helpless.

10. TOUCH NOT THE POISONOUS FIREWATER that robs man of his strength, and makes wise men turn fools. Touch not nor taste any food or drink that robs the body of its power or the spirit of its vision.

11. BE CLEAN, both yourself and the place you dwell in. Bathe every morning in cold water, take the

---

[21] Killing an enemy in time of war was another matter, just as in modern civilization.

[22] In some Tribes, such as the Cheyennes and the Sioux, infidelity on the part of a married woman was considered a crime, worthy of death, or was, at least, grounds for divorce. In the case of the man, the penalty was less severe, as with us. In some other Tribes, more lenient views prevailed.

[23] Bishop Whipple, George Bird Grinnell, and many others tell us that theft was unknown in an Indian camp. Horse-stealing between Tribes was recognized as a kind of manly game, and not at any time considered a crime.

Deer Dancer
by Crisenzio Roybar
of San Ildefonso

Sweat Lodge according to your need, and thus perfect your body; for the body is the sacred temple of the spirit.

12. LOVE YOUR LIFE, PERFECT YOUR LIFE, BEAUTIFY ALL THINGS IN YOUR LIFE: GLORY IN YOUR STRENGTH AND BEAUTY. Rejoice in the fullness of your aliveness. Seek to make your life long and full of service to your people. And prepare

a noble Death Song for the day when you are about to cross the Great Divide.

A MYSTIC AND AN OCCULTIST

Second sight—that is occult vision, or clairvoyance—was widely understood and cultivated by the Indians. All their great leaders were mystics. Sitting Bull was an outstanding example. He commonly induced the trance and the vision by prayer, fasting and lonely vigil.

He realized by observation that alcohol is the great enemy of clairvoyance, and continually preached against it, warning his people that "firewater will rob you of the vision."[24]

"It is well known," says Ohiyesa, "that the American Indian had somehow developed occult power, and although in the latter day there have been many impostors, and, allowing for the variety and weakness of human nature, it is fair to assume that there must have been some even in the old days. Yet there are well-attest-

---

[24] Occult authorities locate the clairvoyant sense in the pineal gland, and warn us that it is quickly atrophied, and the sense obliterated by habitual use of alcohol.

ed instances of remarkable prophecies and other mystic practice."[25]

"I cannot pretend to explain them [these prophecies], but I know that our people possessed remarkable powers of concentration and abstraction, and I sometimes fancy that such nearness to nature as I have described keeps the spirit sensitive to impressions not commonly felt, and in touch with the unseen powers."[26]

"If you would purify your heart," says Wabasha, "and so see clearer the way of the Great Spirit, touch no food for two days or more, according to your strength. For thereby the body is purged, and your spirit hath mastery over the body.

"By prayer and fasting and fixed purpose, you can rule your own spirit, and so have power over all those about you."

Because the body is the soul made visible, we are in this life constructing the soul and the body that will be ours in the next.

By prayer and fasting and high service, we can so raise the quality of our being that we enter the next life with completeness of vision, hearing the Voices, and with knowledge of the Great Mystery.[27]

"The first *hambeday*, or religious retreat, marked an epoch in the life of the youth which may be compared to that of confirmation or conversion in Christian experience. Having first prepared himself by means of the purifying vapor bath, and cast off, as far as possible, all human or fleshly influences, the young man sought out the noblest height, the most commanding summit

[25] Ohiyesa, *The Soul of the Indian*, p. 137.
[26] *Ibid.*, p 163.
[27] "Many of the Indians believed that one may be born more than once; and there were some who claimed to have full knowledge of a former incarnation."—*Ibid.*, p. 167.

in all the surrounding region. Knowing that God sets no value upon material things, he took with him no offerings or sacrifices, other than symbolic objects, such as paints and tobacco. Wishing to appear before Him in all humility, he wore no clothing save his moccasins and breechclout. At the solemn hour of sunrise or sunset, he took up his position, overlooking the glories of earth, and facing the 'Great Mystery,' and there he remained, naked, erect, silent, and motionless, exposed to the elements and forces of His arming, for a night and a day or two days and nights, but rarely longer. Sometimes he would chant a hymn without words, or offer the ceremonial 'filled pipe.' In this holy trance or ecstasy the Indian mystic found his highest happiness, and the motive power of his existence."[28]

THE INDIAN SILENCE[29]

"The first American mingled with his pride a singular humility. Spiritual arrogance was foreign to his nature and teaching. He never claimed that the power of articulate speech was proof of superiority over the dumb creation; on the other hand, it is to him a perilous gift. He believes profoundly in silence—the sign of a perfect equilibrium. Silence is the absolute poise or balance of body, mind, and spirit. The man who preserves his selfhood, ever calm and unshaken by the storms of existence—not a leaf, as it were, astir on the tree; not a ripple upon the surface of shining pool—his, in the mind of the unlettered sage, is the ideal attitude and conduct of life.

---

[28] *Ibid.*, pp. 7-8.
[29] *Ibid.*, pp. 89-90.

"If you ask him, 'What is silence?' he will answer, 'It is the Great Mystery. The holy silence is His voice!' If you ask, 'What are the fruits of silence?' he will say, 'They are self-control, true courage or endurance, patience, dignity, and reverence. Silence is the cornerstone of character.'

"'Guard your tongue in youth,' said the old Chief Wabasha, 'and in age you may mature a thought that will be of service to your people!'"

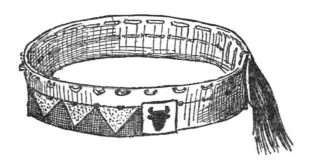

THE DAILY WORSHIP

"In the life of the Indian," says Ohiyesa, the Sioux, "there was only one inevitable duty—the duty of prayer, the daily recognition of the Unseen and Eternal. His daily devotions were more necessary to him than daily food. He wakes at daybreak, puts on his moccasins, and steps down to the water's edge. Here he throws handfuls of clear, cold water into his face, or plunges in bodily. After the bath, he stands erect before the advancing dawn, facing the sun as it dances upon the horizon, and offers his unspoken orison. His mate may precede or follow him in his devotions, but never accompanies him. Each soul must meet the morning sun, the new sweet earth, and the Great Silence alone!"[30]

So also their other prophets: "When you arise in the morning, give thanks for the morning light. Give thanks for your life and strength. Give thanks for your food and give thanks for the joy of living. And if perchance you see no reason for giving thanks, rest assured the fault is in yourself."

Then, continuing the daily round, Ohiyesa says: "When food is taken, the woman murmurs a 'grace' as she lowers the kettle, an act so softly and unobtrusively performed that one who does not know the custom usually fails to catch the whisper: 'Spirit, partake!' As her husband receives the bowl or plate, he likewise murmurs his invocation to the Spirit. When he becomes an old man, he loves to make a notable effort to prove his gratitude. He cuts off the choicest morsel of the meat and casts it into the fire—the purest and most ethereal element."[31]

When ye are assembled in Council, fail not to light in the midst the Fire which is the symbol of the Great Spirit and the sign of His presence.

And light the Sacred Pipe, which is the symbol of Peace, Brotherhood, Council and Prayer, and smoke first to the Great Spirit in Heaven above, then to the Four Winds, His messengers, and to Mother Earth, through whom He furnishes us our food.

And let each Councilor smoke, passing the Pipe in a circle like that of the Sun from east southward to the west.

At the opening of Council, let the Chief arise, light the pipe, and pray: "Wakan Tanka Wakan na kay chin, Chandee eeya paya wo." That is, "Great Spirit, by

---

[30] *Ibid.*, pp. 45-46.
[31] *Ibid.*, pp. 47-48.

this pipe, the symbol of Peace, Council, and Brotherhood, we ask Thee to be with us and bless us tonight."

INDIAN PRAYERS

I

O Great Spirit of my fathers, this is my prayer.
Help me to feel Thine urge and Thy message.
Help me to be just even to those who hate me; and
at all times help me to be kind.
If mine enemy is weak and faltering, help me to the
good thought that I forgive him.
If he surrender, move me to help him as a weak
and needy brother.

II

O Great Spirit of my fathers, help me to wholly void
my heart of fear.
And above all things, O God of my people and of
my soul, help me to be a man.

III

O God, show me the way of wisdom, and give me
strength to follow it without fear.

IV

O Great Spirit, this is my prayer! Grant that fear
may never enter into my heart to be the guide of my
feet.

V

O Great Spirit, make me sufficient to mine own
occasions.

Give to me to mind my own business at all times, and to lose no good opportunity for holding my tongue.

When it is appointed for me to suffer, let me take example from the dear well-bred beasts and go away in solitude to bear my suffering by myself, not troubling others with my complaints.

Help me to win, if win I may, but—and this especially, O Great Spirit—if it be not ordained that I may win, make me at least a good loser.[32]

THE OMAYA TRIBAL PRAYER

*"Wa-kon-da dhe dhu
Wapa-dhin a-ton-he."*

Translated into our tongue: "Father, a needy one stands before Thee. I that sing am he."

---

[32] This prayer, in brief, was inscribed on the wall of King George's study, Buckingham Palace, London.

This noble prayer to God was sung on the Missouri River, we believe, long before Columbus landed, and with the music, words, and attitude just as we of the Woodcraft Way use them today.

During the prayer those assembled stand in a great circle about the fire, with faces and hands raised to heaven. As the final words are sung, hands and heads are bowed to the symbolic fire, and the Chief announces: "With this our council is ended."

HYMN TO TIRAWA (GOD)[33]

This noble Pawnee Hymn to God, recorded by Fletcher, is comparable to the Psalms of David:

I

Tirawa, harken! Mighty one
Above us in blue, silent sky!
We standing wait thy bidding here;
The Mother Corn standing waits,
Waits to serve thee here;
The Mother Corn stands waiting here.

II

Tirawa, harken! Mighty one
Above us in blue, silent sky!
We flying seek thy dwelling there;
The Mother Corn flying goes
Up to seek thee there;
The Mother Corn goes flying up.

---

[33] From the Pawnee Hako (Fletcher), *22nd Ann. Rep. Bur. Eth.*, Part 2, 1904, p. 347.

III

Tirawa, harken ! Mighty one
Above us in blue, silent sky!
We touch upon thy country fair;
The Mother Corn touches there
Upon the border land;
The Mother Corn is touching there.

IV

Tirawa, harken! Mighty one
Above us in blue, silent sky!
The path we reach leads up to thee;
The Mother Corn enters there,
Upward takes her way;
The Mother Corn to thee ascends.

V

Tirawa, harken! Mighty one
Above us in blue, silent sky!
Behold! We in thy dwelling stand;
The Mother Corn, standing there,
Leader now is made;
The Mother Corn is leader made.

VI

Tirawa, harken! Mighty one
Above us in blue, silent sky!
The downward path we take again;
The Mother Corn, leading us,
Doth thy symbol bear;
The Mother Corn with power leads.

BURIAL AND HOPE FOR THE DEAD

The burial ceremonies, the respect for the departed and the belief in a future life are set forth in the practice of many tribes. Catlin, speaking of the Mandans, says: "Whenever a person dies in the Mandan Village, the customary honor and condolence are paid to his remains, and the body is dressed in its best attire, painted, oiled, and supplied with bow and quiver, shield, pipe and tobacco, knife, flint and steel, and food enough to last him a few days on the journey which he is to perform. A fresh buffalo's skin, just taken from the animal's back, is wrapped around the body, and tightly bound and wound with thongs of rawhide from head to foot. Then other robes are soaked in water, till they are quite soft and elastic, which are also bandaged round the body in the same manner, and tied fast with thongs, which are wound with great care and exactness, so as to exclude the action of the air from all parts of the body.

"There is then a separate scaffold erected for it, constructed of four upright posts a little higher than human hands can reach, and on the tops of these are small poles passing around from one post to the others, across which are a number of willow rods just strong enough to support the body, which is laid upon them on its back, with its feet carefully presented towards the rising sun...."

"The traveler…if he will give attention to the respect and devotions that are paid to this sacred place, will draw many a moral deduction that will last him through life; he will learn, at least, that filial, conjugal, and paternal affection are not necessarily the results of civilization; but that the Great Spirit has given them to man in his native state."[34]

The Pueblos and some other Tribes, according to Dr. E. L. Hewett, are strangely indifferent to the body after death. They consider it a mere husk, an empty case, to be disposed of with view only to the comfort of the survivors. The soul that emerged will go on to the next life, and construct for itself a new and better body.

DEATH SONGS

Every Indian in the old days had a Death Song prepared for the time when he knew he was facing the end.
One Indian Chief confided to me that his Death Song was the same as that of the thirty-seven Sioux patriots who were executed at Mankato, Minnesota, in 1862 for seeking to drive the invaders from their country:

> I, Chaska, do sing:
> I care not where my body lies,
> My soul goes marching on.
> I care not where my body lies,
> My soul goes marching on.

When Nanni Chaddi and his four Apache warriors, after four days of starvation, thirst and agony, decided to face and fight rather than surrender to the

---

[34] George Catlin, *Manners, Customs, and Conditions of the North American Indians*, vol. i, p. 89, 1841.

White regiment that had them cornered in a cave, they sang to God:

> Father, we are going out to die.
> For ourselves we grieve not,
> But for those who are left behind.
> Let not fear enter into our hearts.
> We are going out to die.

Then, armed only with arrows and lances, they dashed into the fire of a hundred rifles, and were shot to rags.

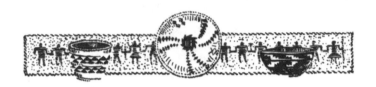

III

THE ANCIENT WAY

A Successful Socialist

Some years ago the Canadian Government made a ruling that no settler who wished to live on a small island would be allowed a homestead claim. The reason given was that no man who wished to live alone can, in the last analysis, be a good citizen.

A good citizen needs near neighbors for himself, for his work, and for his family.

Sociability as a fundamental of human nature is fully recognized in all Indian Tribes—even the nomads—and is the inevitable solution of many of the troubles that are harassing the White race in America.

The Indian was a socialist in the best and literal meaning of the word. The White farmer or hunter might live in a lonely cabin on his farm or on his hunting quest; but the Indian was always found living in a village with his people, either a movable village as among the nomadic Tribes of the Buffalo Plains, or in a farming village as among the Pueblos, or the Mandans, or the Tribes of the upper Missouri.

The Redman's social system was very nearly the same as that instituted by Moses. Catlin remarks the identity of their laws with those of the Israelites, and instances their marriage customs, treatment of sick, burial of dead, mourning, ablutions. "In their feasts, fastings, and sacrificing [he says], they are exceedingly like those ancient people, the Jews."[1]

The highest development of the Indian culture was seen in Central and South America, about the time of the Spanish discovery.

According to Professor G. P. Murdoch,[2] the Inca social system of Peru was communistic, or, as he styles it, strictly one of "State Socialism." Under this system, the weak, the sick and the aged were adequately cared for.

"What marks it indelibly as Socialistic, however, is its system of distribution. It achieved an equilibrium of production and consumption, not through the free interchange of goods, but through State-supervised, periodic distributions of the surplus production....

"It achieved an exceptional measure of law and order, it prevented the waste of national resources, and it eliminated entirely the hazards of poverty and involuntary unemployment."[3]

Avarice, the root of all evil, was impossible, partly because they had no money; also because there was a strongly established public sentiment against any one man having vast possessions. When the fortunes of war or of commerce resulted in one man accumulating a great number of horses, blankets or other property, it was the custom for him to give a feast or potlatch and distribute his surplus among those who had little or none.

Trade was carried on through a system of barter, by sticks or counters. On the Plains, the smallest unit was an arrow, worth ten cents; the next unit was a beaver skin, worth one dollar; the next a buffalo robe, worth

---

[1] Vol. ii, p. 233.

[2] Professor George Peter Murdoch, "The Organization of Inca Society," *Scientific Monthly*, March 1934, pp. 231-39.

[3] *Ibid.*, pp. 238, 239.

five dollars. Sometimes a horse came next with a value of two robes. These varied in different regions. On the Atlantic Coast, wampum or shell money was used.

Although concrete articles were mentioned in these values, they were not necessarily produced, but were merely the names of such values. Usually the barter was completed at once, so there was no hoarding of the sticks or counters used.

FUNDAMENTAL LAWS

No man owns land.[4] The land belongs to the Tribe, which keeps other Tribes off it. A man owns only so much land as he tills, or occupies with his house or his field. When he ceases to occupy or till that land, it goes back to the Tribe, to be allotted to another member.

No man owns the wood of the forest, or the water of the rivers, or the soil of the earth. He did not

---

[4] Fifty years ago, Henry George came from the West, preaching the gospel of national ownership of land. This idea apparently he got from the Indians. In his book on the single tax, he claimed that private ownership of land was the foundation of all misery and poverty among the Whitemen.

make them, they are the harvest of the land that belongs to the whole people; and only so much of them is his as he can gather with his own hands and use in his own home.

The wild plants are under the same law, but a man may claim certain forage crops, such as wild rice, by establishing his owner mark around a reasonable area before it is ripe to cut. Nevertheless, the High Council shall be judge as to the reasonableness of his claim.

If any man shall gather a pile of firewood or buffalo chips or other fuel, or substance, such as clay or stone or poles or willows, and leave on it the mark of his ownership, that mark shall protect it from all who would take it till that season is over. After that, it becomes again tribal property.

No man owns game or wild animals, for these are the produce of the land that belongs to the nation— only so much of them is his as he can effectively and lawfully possess with his own hands. In some cases he may hold the sole right to capture eagles within a limited area.

"Notwithstanding the prodigality of nature and his independence of the cares which beset the modern man, the old Indian was not wasteful of his resources. He picked no more berries than he needed to stay the cravings of his hunger, and scrupulously avoided injuring trees and bushes which bore anything edible. He killed no more game than he needed for himself and his camp, and ate every part of what he did kill. When he built a fire, he used only the fuel that was necessary, and before quitting the spot extinguished the flame with care."[5]

The Tribe alone controls all tribal interests.

[5] F. E. Leupp, *In Redman's Land*, 1914, pp. 66, 67.

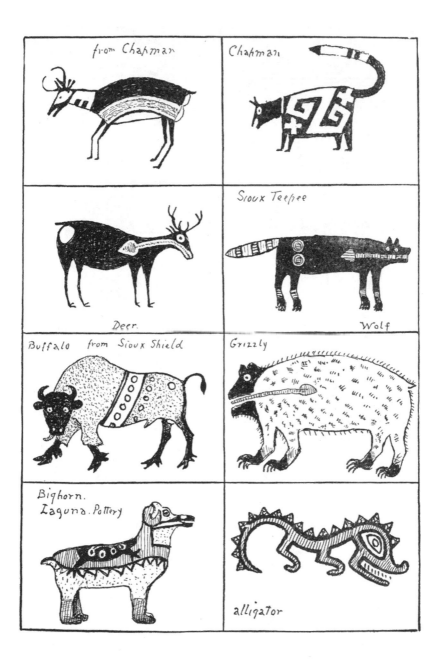

from Chapman

Chapman

Sioux Teepee

Deer.

Wolf

Buffalo from Sioux Shield

Grizzly

Bighorn.
Laguna. Pottery

alligator

Conventional Birds
Pueblo Designs

E.T.S.

The Tribe may give to one family the exclusive right to hunt or gather wood or forage or wild rice or fruit in one tract or range, but the family cannot sell this right, nor can they hire others to hunt or gather for them, lest the hunting be destroyed by overdrain.

If one finds game on the range, and have it in his power, only so much may be killed as he needs and can use. He may not kill for the evil pleasure of killing and wasting.[6]

When a man goes trapping and raids a beaver pond, he must not take all the beaver. He should leave at least a pair to stock again the pond. Leave also the dams and the houses, so that the beaver may recover and again restock the range.

If one find deer in a deer-yard when the snow is deep, he shall kill only so many as he and his people nigh at hand can use. It is a dishonorable thing to kill so much game that it goes to waste. The punishment of those who so behave is that some day they shall suffer starvation.

It is lawful to fire the prairie in fall, or in spring when the grass is dry; for thereby little damage is done, and the grass comes many days sooner and is much better in the springtime afterward. But it is at no time lawful to set the forest afire, for that is a great and lasting calamity to all who dwell therein, whether men or game, and it never recovers itself of the damage.

All men are free and equal, and have a right to the pursuit of happiness in their own way—so only they do not encroach on the same right of others.

---

[6] The late Major James McLaughlin, of the Indian Service, says: "I never have known an Indian to kill a game animal that he did not require for his needs. And I have known few White hunters to stop while there was game to kill."—*My Friend the Indian*, p. 114.

Every man must treat with respect all such things as are sacred to other people, whether he comprehends them or not.

Every man and woman who is in sickness or adversity, or helpless old age, has a right to the protection and support of the Tribe—because in the days of their strength they also contributed to the common weal.

MARRIAGE AND DIVORCE

Every man and woman is expected to marry on coming of age. Celibacy is almost a disgrace, implying in some sort a failure. Marriages are arranged for all, and must not be within one's own clan.[7]

There was but little ceremony at the wedding. The man who desired a certain woman and had secured evidence of her approval sent to the girl's parents a present, proportional to his means. This was not truly wife purchase; it was rather considered compensation for loss of her services.

Marriage was, among the Indians, strictly a civil contract, dissoluble at any time by mutual consent and usually for one of three causes—infelicity, infidelity, or infertility. Divorce was allowed on the same basis as in the Mosaic code: if the man prove a failure as a husband, if the pair are not blessed with children, or serious discord develops, they can quickly have their union dissolved, each being free and expected to marry again. Marital infidelity was rare, because the remedy for discord was so easily within reach.

---

[7] This device seems to have been invented to prevent in-breeding.

THE CHILDREN

Every child is entitled to a home, food, upbringing, and an education—and if so be he has no near kin, then he is a proper and honorable charge on the Tribe.

There was no such thing as an illegitimate child—that is, a child without social standing or legal rights because its parents were unmarried. All were legitimate, and when an unmarried woman had a baby, there never was lack of a kind person ready to offer the little one a home and an adoptive father.

The tender regard of the Indian parent for the children is well known. More than one of their prophets have said: "If your child be wayward, unruly, rebellious, or insolent, do not beat him. Only a brute and a coward would beat a helpless child. Rather discipline him by exclusion from the games with his fellows, and even to fasting till he is brought to see his error. Remember, the sorrow of being an outcast will speedily discipline him into obedience—whereas the wickedness of beating his body will surely result in lifelong hate and indignation against those who have so tortured him."

"The North American Indians are not only affectionately attached, indeed, to their own offspring, but are extremely fond of children in general. They instruct them carefully in their own principles, and train them up with attention in the maxims and habits of their nation. Their system consists chiefly in the influence of example, and impressing upon them the traditional histories of their ancestors.

"When the children act wrong, their parents remonstrate and reprimand, but never chastise them."[8]

Love of their children is a dominant characteristic of the Red race. I never saw an Indian child spanked; I never saw an Indian child spoiled.

The children were the property of the mother until puberty.

STATUS OF WOMEN

Women had votes among the Indians ages before they were accorded the privilege in Europe. They had a voice in all national affairs and could rise to the chieftainship. In many Tribes, the High Chief was a woman. These were called Women Sachems, Rowainers, or Rainbow Women, according to the Tribe to which they belonged.

In most Tribes, the woman is the owner of the home and of the children, and of whatever is in the home. The man owns the horses, cattle, and crops, and whatever he produces or secures with his own hands.

But when game is killed, or crops harvested and brought into the house, they become the property of the wife.

CHASTITY

"With the Indians, perfect chastity was the rule, not the exception. The rule was respected by the man, and he killed his wife if she broke it; and public sentiment ap-

---

[8] John Halkett, *Indians of North America*, 1825, p. 23.

proved his act. Unfaithfulness was an unpardonable sin."[9]

Jonathan Carver, who traveled among the Sioux from 1766 to 1769, says: "Adultery is esteemed by them a heinous crime, and punished with the greatest rigor."[10]

Colonel R. I. Dodge, an Indian fighter, says: "The Cheyenne women are retiring and modest, and for chastity will compare favorably with women of any other nation or people...almost models of purity and chastity."[11]

Major James McLaughlin says that the Sioux "hold nothing more sacred than the purity of a maiden."[12]

These high standards were held among all the great tribes such as the Sioux, the Cheyennes and those who shared their culture. Among these, it was customary to have a Maiden Dance at special times. Only virgins might take part, and anyone was at liberty to challenge the right of such a one to dance—but he must be prepared with absolute proof or his punishment for false charges might be frightful, even death.

In other Tribes, more lenient views prevailed. Yet, among these, all valued the virginity of a woman; and a woman who transgressed was less highly esteemed because she was less likely to be true to the man she married. But there was no public scorn. Unchaste women were not treated as criminals; any more than a Whiteman is made outcast for taking a little too much to drink.

---

[9] John James, *My Experience with Indians*, 1925, pp. 64-65.

[10] *Travels*, 1796, p. 245.

[11] *Hunting-grounds of the Great West*, 1883, p. 302.

[12] *My Friend the Indian*, p. 74.

As Seen by the Missionaries

The Rev. C. Van Dusen, missionary to the Ojibway Indians, writes: "The Indian character, in its unadulterated grandeur, is most admirable and attractive. Before it is polluted by the pernicious example of others—the demoralizing and debasing influence of wicked Whitemen—the genuine North American pagan presents to the world the most noble specimen of the natural man that can be found on the face of the earth."[13]

Bishop Henry Benjamin Whipple, of Minnesota, thus sums up the wild Indian, after intimate knowledge, during a lifetime of association: "The North American Indian is the noblest type of a heathen man on the earth. He recognizes a Great Spirit; he believes in immortality; he has a quick intellect; he is a clear thinker; he is brave and fearless, and, until betrayed, he is true to his plighted faith; he has a passionate love for his children, and counts it a joy to die for his people. Our most terrible wars have been with the noblest types of the Indians and with men who had been the Whiteman's friends. Nicolet said the Sioux were the finest type of wild men he had ever seen."[14]

The Jesuits testify of the Iroquois, 1636: "Hospitals for

---

[13] *The Indian Chief,* 1867, p. 1.

[14] Helen Hunt Jackson, *A Century of Dishonor,* 1909, p. 7.

the poor would be useless among them, because there are no beggars; those who have are so liberal to those who are in want, that everything is enjoyed in common. The whole village must be in distress before any individual is left in necessity."[15]

"In truth," says Father Jerome Lalemant of the Hurons, "their customs are barbarous in a thousand matters; but, after all, in those practices which among them are regarded as evil acts and are condemned by the public, we find without comparison much less disorder [lawlessness] than there is in France, though here the mere shame of having committed the crime is the offender's punishment."[16]

Even stronger is the summary of the Jesuit father, J. F. Lafitau: "They are high-minded and proud; possess a courage equal to every trial; an intrepid valor; the most heroic constancy under torments, and an equanimity which neither misfortunes nor reverses can shake. Toward each other, they behave with a natural politeness and attention, entertaining a high respect for the aged, and a consideration for their equals which appears scarcely reconcilable with that freedom and independence of which they are so jealous."[17]

"They never permit themselves to indulge in passion, but always from a sense of honor and greatness of soul, appear masters of themselves."[18]

In the summer of 1912, I met Father A. M. Beede, a Jesuit missionary at Standing Rock, Fort Yates, North Dakota. He had gone there twenty-five years before, an enthusiastic young religionist, convinced that the highest calling on earth was that of missionary—his noblest

[15] *Ibid.*, p. 379.

[16] *Relation des jésuites*, 1644-5, vol. 28, p. 63, Thwaite's edition.

[17] *Moeurs des sauvages américains*, 1724, vol. 1, p. 106.

[18] *Ibid.*, pp. 105-6.

triumph would be the conversion of these Indians to his particular form of Christianity.

He began, as all sincere and devoted missionaries do, by learning the language and also studying the philosophy of the people he hoped to influence.

When I first saw him he had ceased to call them "benighted heathens" and was already admitting that they were a noble race with high standards of religion and ethics.

Not long afterwards he admitted to me that the Medicine Lodge of the Sioux Nation was "a true Church of God, and we have no right to stamp it out."

When I went to Standing Rock (Fort Yates, N.D.) with a dozen of my students in 1927, I sought for Father Beede, but found him not. Instead I found him as "Lawyer Beede" and heard the story of a noble and sincere messenger.

"Yes," he said, "I realized that the Sioux were worshippers of the one true God, and their religion was one of truth and kindness. They do not need a missionary, but they do need a lawyer to defend them in the Courts.

"So I abandoned my role as missionary and studied law. After some years I was admitted to the bar of North Dakota, and now I am their permanent official advocate in all cases involving Indians that come into Court.

"Of course the missionaries have unfrocked me, and the Indian agents hate me. The Indians can pay me little or nothing for my services. I live in a little cabin built by myself and cook my own meals.

"But I glory in the fact that I am devoting the last of my days and my strength to the service of this noble, downtrodden Race."

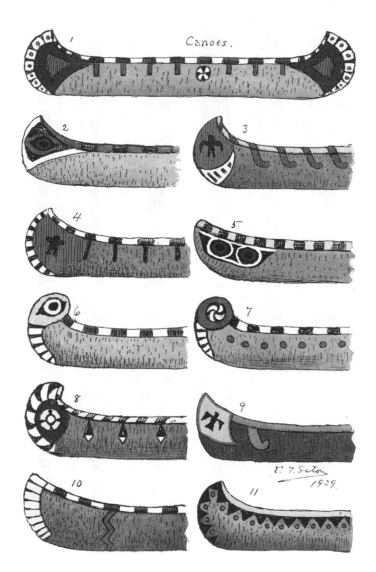

Canoes.

E. T. Seton
1929.

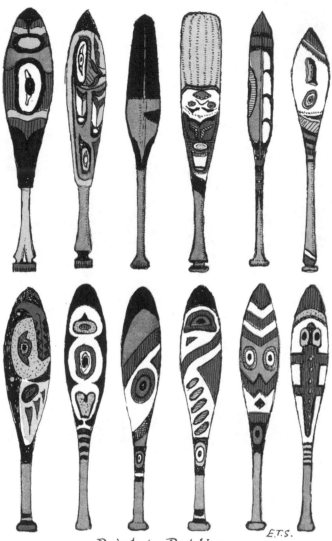

Painted Paddles

E.T.S.

As Seen by the Soldiers

Long after Lafitau, the judicial Morgan, in his *League of the Iroquois,* says: "In legislation, in eloquence, in fortitude, and in military sagacity, they [the Iroquois] had no equals.

"Crimes and offences were so infrequent, under their social system, that the Iroquois can scarcely be said to have had a criminal code."[19]

"On all occasions, and at whatever price, the Iroquois spoke the truth, without fear and without hesitation."[20]

"There are few people so generous as the Indians. In their religious and war ceremonies, at their feasts, festivals, and funerals, the widows and orphans, the poor and needy are always thought of; not only thought of ... but their poverty and necessity are relieved.

"I have seen Whitemen reduced to the last 'hardtack,' with only tobacco enough for two smokes, and with no immediate prospect of anything better than horse meat 'straight.' A portion of the hard bread was hidden away, and the smokes were taken in secret. An Indian, undemoralized by contact with the Whites, under similar circumstances, would divide down to the last morsel."[21]

"No matter how great the scarcity of food might be, so long as there was any remaining in the lodge, the visitor received his share without grudging."[22]

---

[19] Lewis Henry Morgan, *League of the Ho-dé-no-sau-nee or Iroquois,* p. 55.

[20] *Ibid.,* p. 330.

[21] Captain W. Philo Clark, *Sign Language,* 1884, pp. 185, 186.

[22] George Bird Grinnell, *The North American Indians of To-day,* 1900, p. 9.

Captain John G. Bourke, who spent most of his active life as an Indian fighter, and who, by training, was an Indian hater, was at last, even in the horror of an Indian-crushing campaign, compelled to admit: "The American Indian, born free as the eagle, would not tolerate restraint, would not brook injustice; therefore, the restraint imposed must be manifestly for his benefit, and the government to which he was subjected must be eminently one of kindness, mercy and absolute justice, without necessarily degenerating into weakness. The American Indian despises a liar. The American Indian is the most generous of mortals; at all his dances and feasts, the widow and the orphan are the first to be remembered."[23]

On December 15, 1915, Buffalo Bill dined with me in Washington, D.C. It happened to be our last meeting, and his last words deeply impressed me. We were talking of the Indians, and Bill said, "I never led an expedition against the Indians but I was ashamed of myself, ashamed of my government, and ashamed of my flag; for they were always in the right and we were always in the wrong. They never broke a treaty, and we never kept one."

On February 8, 1935, at Douglas, Arizona, I met Neil Erickson, who was a scout under General Crook and again under General Miles during the two campaigns against Victorio and Geronimo. After reviving the ancient memories, he said and dictated for print: "If I had known then what I know now about Indian character, I would have deserted from the American army and joined up with the Apaches."

General N. A. Miles himself described the Indians as "the most heroic race the world has ever seen."

---

[23] Captain John G. Bourke, *On the Border with Crook*, 1892, p. 226.

As Seen by Our Wise Men

Dr. Edgar L. Hewett has publicly stated many times:
"There can be no question that the Redman had evolved
a better civilization than our own. Its one weakness was
in the fact that it did not carry the mastery of metals."
This idea is fully set forth in the pages of his book.[24] On

---

[24] *Ancient Life in the American Southwest,* 1930.

page 31 he adds, "In aesthetic, ethical, and social culture, the Indians surpassed their conquerors." And on page 42: "It is to the glory of the American Indian race that it developed a type of government entirely different from that of the European and more effective. The welfare of the people was the supreme end of government."

Professor C. A. Nichols, of the Southwestern University, Georgetown, Texas, a profound student of Indian life, said to me sadly, in reference to the destruction of the primitive Indian: "I am afraid we have stamped out a system that was producing men who, taken all round, were better than ourselves" (November 11, 1911).

Thus these soldiers and travelers, with scarcely a dissentient voice, proclaimed that the Redman, in the free enjoyment of his life and religion, was brave, clean, kind, religious, and reverent; temperate and unsordid, untainted by avarice, dignified, courteous, truthful, and honest; the soul of honor, and gifted with a physique that represents the highest bodily development of which the world has record.

Witchcraft Is a Crime

The belief in witchcraft was widely spread among the Indians. Their ideas and attitude toward it were much like those announced by Moses. The subject is obscure and perplexing. There are not lacking those who believe in witchcraft as the hypnotic power of a strong will over a weaker. Decrepit old women are the unlikeliest persons in the world to have such power.

The subject is not exhausted nor is the idea exploded. The valid legal plea of "undue influence" comes properly under this head.

MEDICINE MEN OR SHAMANS

The Medicine Men or Shamans were healers, as well as wise men. While these were supposed to know surgery as well as medicine, their knowledge was very superficial and quite empirical. Their practice was largely with a spiritual approach, as indeed were most Indian ways of life.

They had no knowledge of our modern science of biochemistry, but they understood and worked largely with massage, sweat baths, mud baths, mineral springs, decoctions of barks, sun rays, pinewood air and smoke, and faith cure. They had, moreover, much knowledge of the occult properties of plants, a knowledge which, alas, is being allowed to die out. In treatment of snakebite, for instance, some had and still have a sovereign remedy.

We owe to the ancient Peruvians our knowledge and use of such drugs as cocaine, quinine, cascara, ipecac, tolu, cola, and the like.[25]

PUNISHMENTS FOR CRIME

The Indians had no written speech and no codification of their laws. The laws were purely traditional, and the punishment for breach of the same was meted out by the Chief and the High Council, or sometimes the Chief alone. In some cases, the aggrieved party was encouraged to take the law into his own hands.

In all cases, public opinion was the most important influence in appraising a crime. In some cases, compensatory damages were imposed on the delinquent; in rare cases, physical punishment; in extreme cases, death or ostracism.

[25] Dr. F. W. Hodge, in personal correspondence.

Dog Soldiers

Each of the great Plains tribes had a Lodge of Dog Soldiers, who were the police. They took orders from the Chief, and were sworn to "walk straight," that is, obey him, without regard for any personal consequences.

Torture of Prisioners and Scalping

The cruelest folk recorded in history were the Christians of the Middle Ages. One notorious preacher and leader of a Christian Church decoyed his rival preacher into a trap, and not only condemned him to be burned alive, but deliberately selected green wood that the agony might thereby be prolonged.

The diabolical ingenuity of the European torturers was not satisfied by the fiery death, preceded by long slow mutilation; but mental agonies were invented as well, that could and did prolong the horror for weeks and months. The official records of the Holy Inquisition announce proudly that they burned alive 300,000 human beings because they differed from them in religious belief.[26]

---

[26] "This holy office...immolating on its flaming piles more than three hundred thousand victims!"—*The History of the Inquisition of Spain*, by F. Juan Antonio Llorente, former Secretary of the Inquisition, 1843, p. 5.

All historic evidence of value makes it clear that in general the Indians were originally the kindest of people, and torture of prisoners was practically unknown until introduced and made general by the White invaders.[27] We have full records of this introduction by the Christian Pilgrim Fathers in New England and by the Christian Spaniards in Mexico.

Nevertheless there can be no doubt that in primitive days, the Iroquois, the Hurons, the Abnaki and some other Tribes did occasionally torture a prisoner taken in war—either because he was a notorious enemy who had caused them great and terrible losses, or because he directly challenged them to do so—that he might demonstrate his fortitude and defiance to the last.

Among the Christian nations of Europe it was the usual thing to torture all prisoners.

During the War of 1812, both the English under General Proctor and the Americans under General Wayne were following their custom of torturing their prisoners. But in the English army it was stopped by the great Indian Tecumseh, who denounced as cowards any who would torture a helpless captive. When Proctor objected that it was customary, and the men must be amused, Tecumseh challenged Proctor to mortal combat, man to man, whereupon Proctor backed down like the poltroon he was.

Scalping a warrior killed in battle was an established custom in many Tribes; but how much cleaner and better than the Whiteman's custom of putting the

---

[27] Captain W. Philo Clark, discussing the Plains Indians, especially the Cheyennes, says: "There is no good evidence that captives have been burned at the stake, flayed alive or any other excruciating torture inflicted on persons captured by these fierce, war-loving and enterprising barbarians."—*Sign Language*, p. 106.

dead man's head on a pole, that its agonized expression might long be enjoyed by the victor.[28]

It is well known that the Whites did as much scalping as the Indians during the Indian wars, though the fact is commonly omitted from our school readers.

It was from the Puritan Pilgrim Fathers that the Massachusetts Indians learned to scalp their enemies (Hodge).

[28] Dr. F. W. Hodge says, see J. P. Dunn, *Massacres of the Mountains, Christian Atrocities toward Apaches.* Also *The History of James Kirker, the Apache Scalp Hunter.* See also *The Scalp Hunters,* by Captain Mayne Reid.

IV

BY THEIR FRUITS YE SHALL KNOW THEM

Physique

All historians, hostile or friendly, admit the Indian to have been the finest type of physical manhood the world has ever known. None but the best, the picked, chosen and trained of the Whites, had any chance with him.

The Redman's approach to all life and thought was spiritual. The interdependence of body and soul is thus summed up by Ohiyesa in his inspiring account of the religion of his people, the Dakotas: "The moment that man conceived of a perfect body, supple, symmetrical, graceful, and enduring—in that moment he had laid the foundation of a moral life. No man can hope to maintain such a temple of the spirit beyond the period of adolescence unless he is able to curb his indulgence in the pleasures of the senses. Upon this truth, the Indian built a rigid system of physical training, a social and moral code that was the law of his life.

"There was aroused in him as a child a high ideal of manly strength and beauty, the attainment of which must depend upon strict temperance in eating and in the sexual relation, together with severe and persistent exercise. He desired to be a worthy link in the generations, and that he might not destroy by his weakness that vigor and purity of blood which had been achieved at the cost of so much self-denial by a long line of ancestors.

"He was required to fast from time to time for short periods, and to work off his superfluous energy by means of hard running, swimming, and the vapor bath. The bodily fatigue thus induced, especially when coupled with a reduced diet, is a reliable cure for undue sexual desires."[1]

Speaking of the Iroquois in primitive condition, Brinton says that physically "they were unsurpassed by any on the continent, and I may even say by any other people in the world."[2]

The most famous runner of ancient Greece was Pheidippides, whose record run from Athens to Sparta was 140 miles in 36 hours. Among our Indians, such a feat would have been considered very second-rate. In 1882, at Fort Ellice, I saw a young Cree who, on foot, had just brought in dispatches from Fort Qu' Appelle (125 miles away) in 25 hours. It created almost no comment. I heard little from the traders but cool remarks like, "A good boy," "pretty good run." It was obviously a very usual exploit, among Indians.

The two Indian runners, Thomas Zafiro and Leonicio San Miguel, ran 62½ miles, i.e. from Pachuca to Mexico City, in 9 hours, 37 minutes, November 8, 1926, according to the El Paso *Times*, February 14, 1932. This was 9¼ minutes to the mile.

The Zunis have a race called, "Kicked Stick." In this, the contestants each kick a stick before them as they run. Dr. F. W. Hodge tells me that there is a record of 20 miles covered in 2 hours by one of the kickers.

---

[1] Ohiyesa, *The Soul of the Indian*, pp. 90-2.
[2] Dr. Daniel G. Brinton, *The American Race*, 1891, p. 82.

The Tarahumare mail carrier runs 70 miles a day, every day in the week, carrying a heavy mailbag, and he doesn't know that he is doing an exploit.

In addition we are told: "The Tarahumare mail carrier from Chihuahua to Batopiles, Mexico, runs regularly more than 500 miles a week; a Hopi messenger has been known to run 120 miles in 15 hours."[3]

The Arizona Indians are known to run down deer by sheer endurance, and every student of Southwestern history will remember that Coronado's mounted men were unable to overtake the natives when in the hill country, such was their speed and activity on foot.

Running Antelope, Chief among the Hunkpapa Sioux, was famous as an orator and a pictographic artist. He was also a wonderful runner.

"When this Indian was a boy, he ran down and caught an adult antelope in a straight-away race lasting 5 hours, and his people considered this so great a feat that they rechristened him accordingly."[4]

We know that Whitemen's ways, vice, and diseases have robbed the Indians of much of their former physique, according to Dr. Daniel G. Brinton.[5] And yet—"The five companies (500 men) recruited from the Iroquois of New York and Canada, during the Civil War,

---

[3] *Handbook of American Indians*, Part II, 1910, p. 802.

[4] Colonel G. O. Shields, *The Blanket Indian*, 1921, p. 121.

[5] *The American Race*.

stood first on the list among all the recruits of our army, for height, vigor, and corporeal symmetry."[6]

The wonderful work of the Carlisle Indian School football team is a familiar example of what is meant by Indian physique, even at this late date, when the different life has done so much to bring them low.

In 1912, the all-round athletic championship of the world was won at the Olympic Games by James Thorpe, a Carlisle Indian. He was, at best, the pick of 300,000, while against him were Whitemen, the pick of 300,000,000.

A corollary of their muscular perfection was the marvelous nerve of the race.

"The tenacity of life of an Indian, the amount of lead he will carry off, indicates a nervous system so dull as to class him rather with brutes than man. The shock or blow of a bullet will ordinarily paralyze so many nerves and muscles of a Whiteman as to knock him down, even though not striking a vital part. The Indian gives no heed to such wounds, and to drop him in his tracks, the bullet must reach the brain, the heart, or the spine. I have myself seen an Indian go off with two bullets through his body, within an inch or two of the spine, the only effect of which was to cause him to change his gait from a run to a dignified walk."[7]

Dr. Hewett says: "In bodily proportions, color, gesture, dignity of bearing, the race is incomparable. It was free from our infectious scourges, tuberculosis, and syphilis, and the resulting physical deformities and

[6] George Bird Grinnell, *The North American Indians of To-day*, p. 56.
[7] Colonel R. I. Dodge, *Our Wild Indians*, p. 440.

mental degeneracies. It was probably free from leprosy, scrofula, and cancer, and it is safe to say that nervous prostration was unknown to the Indian."[8]

Grinnell says: "The struggle for existence weeded out the weak and the sickly, the slow and the stupid, and created a race physically perfect and mentally fitted to cope with the conditions which they were forced to meet, so long as they were left to themselves."[9]

With an equipment of courage, wood wisdom, strength, endurance, wonderful physique, and speed, we can understand and accept Colonel R. I. Dodge's estimate of the Red Indian as the "finest natural soldier in the world."[10]

CLEANLINESS

Alexander Henry II, a fur and whisky trader, who did his share in degrading the early Indians, and did not love them, admits of the Mandans, in 1806: "Both men and women make it a rule to go down to the river and wash every morning and evening."[11]

"These people, like their neighbors [the Sioux, the Crow, and the Cheyennes] have the custom of washing, morning and evening."[12]

Catlin, after eight years in their lodges (1832-40) says that, notwithstanding many exceptions, among the wild Indians the "strictest regard to decency and cleanliness and elegance of dress is observed, and there are

---

[8] *Ancient Life in the American Southwest*, p. 24.

[9] *The North American Indians of To-day*, p. 7.

[10] *Our Wild Indians*, p. 489.

[11] *Journal*, vol. i, 1897, p. 325.

[12] *Ibid.*, p. 348.

few people, perhaps, who take more pains to keep their persons neat and cleanly, than they do."[13]

"In their bathing and ablutions at all seasons of the year, as a part of their religious observances—having separate places for men and women to perform these immersions—they resemble again the Jews."[14]

Here is a paragraph by J. O. Dorsey on Omaha cleanliness: "The Omahas generally bathe (*hica*) every day in warm weather, early in the morning and at night. Some who wish to do so, bathe also at noon. Jackson, a member of the Elk gens, bathes every day, even in winter. He breaks a hole in the ice on the Missouri River and bathes, or else he rubs snow over his body. In winter the Omahas heat water in a kettle and wash themselves (*kigcija*).... The Ponkas used to bathe in the Missouri every day."[15]

Every Indian village in the old days had a Turkish bath, as we call it—a "Sweat Lodge," as they say—used as a cure for coughs, colds, and inflammatory rheumatism, etc. Catlin describes this in great detail, and says: "I allude to their vapor baths, or *sudatories*, of which each village has several, and which seems to be a kind of public property—accessible to all, and resorted to by all, male and female, old and young, sick and well."[16]

BRAVERY

Old-time travelers and modern Indian fighters agree that there was no braver man on earth, alive or in histo-

---

[13] *Manners, Customs, and Conditions of the North American Indians*, vol. i, p. 96.

[14] *Ibid.*, vol. ii, p. 233.

[15] Dorsey, *3rd Ann. Rep. Bur. Eth.*, 1884, p. 269.

[16] *Manners, Customs, and Conditions of the North American Indians*, vol. i, p. 97.

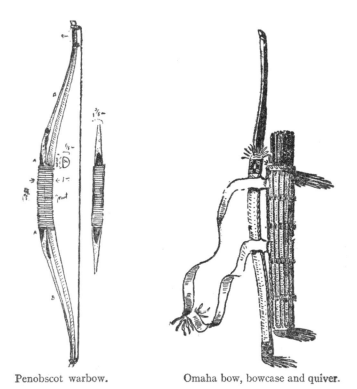

Penobscot warbow.   Omaha bow, bowcase and quiver.

ry, than the Redman. Courage was the virtue he chiefly honored. The purpose of his whole life and training was to make him calm, fearless and efficient in every possible stress or situation.

Father Lafitau said of the Indians of Lower Canada in 1724: "They are high-minded and proud; possess a courage equal to every trial; an intrepid valor; the most heroic constancy under torments, and an equanimity which neither misfortune nor reverses can shake."[17]

"An Indian meets death, when it approaches him in his hut, with the same resolution he has often faced

---

[17] *Moeurs des sauvages américains*, vol. i, p. 106.

it in the field. His indifference relative to this important article, which is the source of so many apprehensions to almost every other nation, is truly admirable. When his fate is pronounced by the physician, and it remains no longer uncertain, he harangues those about him with the greatest composure."[18]

Or he sings the Death Song he has prepared for this very occasion.

"The greatest insult that can be offered to an Indian, is to doubt his courage."[19]

"These savages are possessed with many heroic qualities, and bear every species of misfortune with a degree of fortitude which has not been outdone by any of the ancient heroes either of Greece or of Rome."[20]

"The Indians," writes Lafitau, "seem to prepare themselves for this [fortitude] from the most tender age. Their children have been observed to press their naked arms against each other and put burning cinders between them, defying each other's fortitude in bearing the pain which the fire occasioned. I myself saw a child five or six years old, who, having been severely burnt by some boiling water accidentally thrown upon it, sang its Death Song with the most extraordinary constancy every time they dressed the sores, although suffering the most severe pain."[21]

"With the Indian, courage is absolute self-control. The truly brave man, we contend, yields neither to fear nor anger, desire nor agony. He is at all times master of himself. His courage rises to the heights of chivalry, patriotism, and real heroism.

[18] Jonathan Carver, *Travels*, 1766-69, p. 261.

[19] J. D. Hunter, *Captivity Among the American Indians*, 1798-1816, p. 301.

[20] Jonathan Carver, *Travels*, 1766-69, pp. 221-22.

[21] *Moeurs des sauvages américains*, vol. iv, chap. i.

"'Let neither cold, hunger, nor pain, nor the fear of them, neither the bristling teeth of danger nor the very jaws of death itself, prevent you from doing a good deed,' said an old Chief to a scout who was about to seek the buffalo in midwinter for the relief of a starving people."[22]

None of us is likely to question the Redman's prowess when we remember, for example, that Black Hawk with 40 warriors utterly routed 270 American riflemen in 1832; Chief Joseph in 1877, with inferior weapons, and encumbered with women and children, beat the American soldiers over and over again with double his number; and in 1878 Dull Knife with 69 warriors, fought and defied 2,000 American troops for over four months.

In 1885-86, Geronimo, the Apache Chief, with only 35 men, and no base of supplies, fought off 5,000 regular United States troops, 500 Indian auxiliaries, and a company of Border Scouts, for 18 months, during which time he lost only 6 warriors, but killed a couple hundred of his enemy.

Finally General Nelson A. Miles says: "History can show no parallel to the heroism and fortitude of the American Indians in the 200 years fight during which they contested inch by inch the possession of their country against a foe infinitely better equipped, with inexhaustible resources, and in overwhelming numbers. Had they been equal in numbers, history might have had a very different story to tell."[23]

---

[22] Ohiyesa, *The Soul of the Indian,* p. 115.

[23] Personal letter, February 16, 1912.

CHEERFULNESS

Nothing seems to anger the educated Indian today more than the oft-repeated absurdity that his race was of a gloomy, silent nature. Anyone that has ever been in an Indian village knows what a scene of joy and good cheer it normally was. In every such gathering there was always at least one recognized fun maker, who led them all in joke and hilarious jest. Their songs, their speeches, their fairy tales are full of fun and dry satire. The reports of the Bureau of American Ethnology sufficiently set forth these facts.

Ohiyesa, the Sioux, says on this subject: "There is scarcely anything so exasperating to me as the idea that the natives of this country have no sense of humor and no faculty for mirth. This phase of their character is well understood by those whose fortune or misfortune it has been to live among them, day in and day out, at their homes. I don't believe I ever heard a real hearty laugh away from the Indians' fireside. I have often spent an entire evening in laughter with them, until I could laugh no more. There are evenings when the recognized wit or storyteller of the village gives a free entertainment which keeps the rest of the community in a convulsive state until he leaves them. However, Indian humor consists as much in the gestures and inflections of the voice as in words, and is really untranslatable."[24]

And, again, Grinnell: "The common belief that the Indian is stoical, stolid, and sullen, is altogether erroneous. They are really a merry people, good-natured and jocular, usually ready to laugh at an amusing incident or a joke, with a simple mirth that reminds one of children."[25]

[24] *Indian Boyhood*, 1902, p. 267.
[25] *The North American Indians of To-day*, p. 9.

Ernest Thompson Seton, 1927

Julia M. Seton

Seton laying the cornerstone of the first Boy Scout building in the world,
Baltimore, 1911

Rearview of the Seton house in ruins, Scotland, 1790

The house where Seton was born,
South Shields, England

Seton at two years of age, with father
and mother

Seton, aged 17

Seton at easel, aged 14

Seton, 1896

Seton, 1921

Seton, 1930

Seton, 1936

Julia and Ernest Thompson Seton, 1946

Seton at Standing Rock Village, 1903

Seton teaching fire-making, 1903

Catch-the-Bear, Julia M. Seton, and
Gray Whirlwind

Callous Legs, Mato-Ska (Seton),
Frank Zahn, and Gray Whirlwind

Gray Whirlwind conversing with Seton in sign language

Seton, with three Blackfeet Indians, demonstrating how to start a fire using a bow and a stick

"The Spirit of Woodcraft"
Published on several occasions by Seton to represent the
spirit of the American Indian

Buffalo Dancers.
from Drawing
by Thos. Vigil of Tesuque

Colonel R. I. Dodge, says: "The Indians are habit-
ually and universally the happiest people I ever saw."[26]

HONESTY

Catlin says: "As evidence of... their honesty and honor,
I have roamed about, from time to time, during seven

[26] *Our Wild Indians*, p. 248.

or eight years, visiting and associating with some three or four hundred thousand of these people, under an almost infinite variety of circumstances;...and under all these circumstances of exposure, no Indian ever betrayed me, struck me a blow, or stole from me a shilling's worth of my property, that I am aware of."[27]

"Among the individuals of some tribes or nations, theft is a crime scarcely known."[28]

"As a rule, they kept their promises to me with wonderful fidelity, often putting themselves to extraordinary exertion and peril" (General O. O. Howard).[29]

"If he gives you his word that he [the Indian] will do a thing, you may safely stake your all on his fulfillment of his promise."[30]

Every traveler among the highly developed tribes of the Plains Indians tells a similar story; even that rollicking old cut-throat, Alexander Henry II, says after fifteen years among the wild Indians: "I have been frequently fired at by them and have had several narrow escapes for my life. But I am happy to say they never pillaged me to the value of a needle."[31]

Grand Coup for taking Scalp in Enemy's Camp

C. C. for slapping his face

Coup for Stealing his Horse

---

[27] *Manners, Customs, and Conditions of the North American Indians*, vol. i, pp. 9-10.

[28] J. D. Hunter, *Captivity Among the American Indians*, 1798-1816, p. 300.

[29] Leupp, *In Redman's Land*, p. 86.

[30] *Ibid.*, p. 128.

[31] *Journal*, 1799-1814, p. 452.

"They were friendly in their dispositions, honest to the most scrupulous degree in their intercourse with the Whiteman."[32]

In my own travels in the far North, 1907, I found the Indians tainted with many White vices, and in many respects degenerated; but I also found them absolutely honest, and I left valuable property hung in trees for months, without fear, knowing that no wild Indian would touch it.

There is a story told me by Bishop Whipple: He was leaving his cabin, with its valuable contents, to be gone some months, and sought some way of rendering all robber proof. His Indian guide then said: "Why, Brother, leave it open. Have no fear. There is not a Whiteman within a hundred miles!"

On the road to a certain large Ojibway Indian village in 1904, I lost a considerable roll of bills. My friend, the Whiteman in charge, said: "If an Indian finds it, you will have it again within an hour; if a Whiteman finds it, you will never see it again, for White folk are very weak, when it comes to property matters."

Many years ago (1912) when I was at Standing Rock, N.D., Father Bernard, the missionary, was showing me the church that he and his brethren had built some twenty-five years before, and remarked, "When we first used this church, though it contained much property more or less valuable, we could leave it open all the time without fear, for we were dealing with the old-time Indians who were at all times strictly honest. But now that the younger generation are coming back from your Indian schools in the East, where they have been 'made over into Whitemen,' we have to padlock doors and windows, night and day."

---

[32] Washington Irving, *The Adventures of Captain Bonneville*, 1837, p. 200.

The Hudson's Bay Company officials in Canada assured me on many occasions that their instructions from headquarters were: "Give as much as two years' credit to a wild pagan Indian; but as soon as he cuts his hair, and pretends he is civilized, don't trust him, even overnight."

Finally, to cover the far Southwest, I found that the experience of most travelers agrees with the following: "I lived among the wild Indians for eighteen years (1872-1889); I know the Apaches, the Navajos, the Utes, and the Pueblos, and I never knew a dishonest Indian."[33]

KINDNESS

At every first meeting of Red men and Whites, the Whites were inferior in numbers, and yet were received with the utmost kindness, until they treacherously betrayed those who had helped and harbored them.

Even Christopher Columbus, blind and burnt up with avarice as he was, and soul-poisoned with superstition and contempt for an alien race, yet had fairness to write home to his royal accomplices in crime, the King and Queen of Spain: "I swear to your Majesties that there is not a better people in the world than these; more affectionate, affable, or mild. They love their neighbors as themselves, and they always speak smilingly."[34]

Precisely the same situation appeared when the Pilgrim Fathers began to colonize New England, and when the Virginian colonists landed farther south.

Yet in every case (except that of William Penn),

[33] Robert A. Widenmann, West Haverstraw, N.Y., in a personal letter.

[34] George Catlin, *Manners, Customs, and Conditions of the North American Indians*, vol. ii, p. 246.

Drums & Shields

E. T. Seton

as the colonists grew stronger, they turned on their kind protectors and robbed and murdered without mercy, compunction, or restraint.

In the terrible history of the Donner expedition that tried to cross the Plains and the mountains of California in 1846, we have a harrowing and disgusting picture of the way in which these Christians reviled, hated, harried, robbed and *devoured* each other. They were starving, broken, frost-burnt, ready to kill each other for some trifling advantage.

Then the man, William H. Eddy, who records the horrible story, tells how he, in trying to escape, came to an Indian village, distressed and snowbound in the high Sierras. His reception there by a young Indian is thus related: "My feet were in very bad condition—though no worse than those of my companions. The frosted flesh had broken into deep cracks which refused to heal and continually oozed blood and watery matter.

"The young Indian washed them thoroughly and with the utmost gentleness, speaking softly all the time in tones which indicated his sincere sympathy. The woman carried away the rags and rinsed them clean of the encrusted blood and accumulated filth. No hope of reward could have impelled that act. It was promoted by an inherent nobility and a desire to succor a fellow human whose condition was even more miserable than his own."[35]

Countless similar incidents are on record from earliest times to the present; and yet "the most shameful chapter of American history is that in which is recorded the account of our dealings with the Indians. The story of our Government's intercourse with this race is an unbroken narrative of injustice, fraud and robbery."[36]

---

[35] Bimey, *Grim Journey*, 1934, pp. 150-60.

[36] George Bird Grinnell, *Blackfoot Lodge Tales*, 1892, p. ix.

Abraham Lincoln while President said: "If I live, this accursed system of robbery and shame in our treatment of the Indians shall be reformed."

A characteristic record of the seventeenth century appears on a Puritan's gravestone as follows:

Sacred to the Memory
of
Lynn S. Love
who, during his life time, killed 98 Indians
that had been delivered into his hands by
the Lord. He had hoped to make it 100 before
the year ended when he fell asleep in
the arms of Jesus in his home, in N. Y. State.

CONCEPT OF PEACE

In spite of their readiness for engaging in war when necessary, the Indians had a deeper conception of the fundamental basis of peace than has been generally understood.

In some degree, the meaning was inherent in all tribes, but in the famous Iroquois Confederacy, we find the perfection of the principle.

The vast portion of the continent under their power was surely not held by force alone, for never were there more than 15,000 members, counting men, women and children.

In his *White Roots of Peace*, Paul A. W. Wallace (pp. 3-4) ably expounds the situation. "It was by statesmanship," he says, "by a profound understanding of the principles of peace itself. They knew that any real peace must be based on justice and a healthy reasonableness. They knew also that peace will endure only if men recognize the sovereignty of a common law and are prepared to back that law with force—not chiefly for the purpose

71

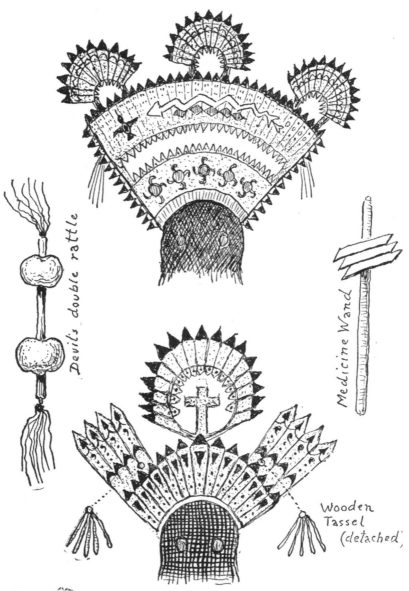

Devils double rattle

Medicine Wand

Wooden
Tassel
(detached)

Head-dresses, & Wands for Devil Dance. E.T.S.

of punishing those who have disturbed the peace, but rather for the purpose of preventing such disturbance by letting all men know, *in advance* of any contingency, that the law will certainly prevail.

"Behind their statesmanship lay a will to peace among the people, without which all the wisdom of their chiefs gathered in the Great Council at Onon-daga would have been futile. It was in the handling of this problem, how to maintain a popular will to peace, that the Iroquois made their greatest contribution to government—a contribution that it may be profitable for us to examine today, since now there is no greater problem confronting global statesmanship than that of maintaining this popular will to peace despite increasing tensions in an ever-more-narrowly-jostling world society....

"They were better in practice than in theory. Their religion was sounder than their theology, their political institutions maturer than their political science. The only science in which they excelled was that of human relationships.

"Peace was not, as they conceived it, a negative thing, the mere absence of war or an interval between wars, to be recognized only as the stepchild of the law— as unfortunately has been the case with most Western peoples, among whom the laws of peace, in the international field, have been recognized by jurists as an afterthought to the laws of war.

"To the Iroquois, peace *was* the law. They used the same word for both. Peace (the Law) was righteousness in action, the practice of justice between individuals and nations. If they ever recognized it as a mystic presence ... they found it not in some imagined retreat from the world, but in human institutions, especially in a good government. Their own Confederacy, which they named the Great Peace, was sacred. The chiefs who administered the League were their priests.

"In their thought, peace was so inseparable from the life of man that they had no separate term by which to denominate it. It was thought of and spoken of in terms of its component elements: as Health (soundness of body and sanity of mind), Law (justice codified to meet particular cases), and Authority (which gives confidence that justice will prevail).

"Peace was a way of life, characterized by wisdom and graciousness.

"Their symbol for this Peace was a Tree, and the Tree had roots in the earth....

"Like the spires of our churches, the Great White Pine which 'pierces the sky' and 'reaches the sun,' lifted the thoughts of the Iroquois to the meanings of peace—the Good News which they believed the Great Spirit... had sent Deganawidah [the promulgator of the League] to impart to them.

"In general, the Tree signified the Law, that is, the constitution, which expressed the terms of their union. But there were other important elements in the symbol.

"The Branches signified shelter, the protection and security that people found in union under the shadow of the Law.

"The Roots, which stretched to the four quarters of the earth, signified the extensions of the Law, the Peace, to embrace all mankind. Other nations, not yet members of the League, would see these roots as they grew outward, and, if they were people of goodwill would desire to follow them to their source and take shelter with others under the Tree.

"The Eagle That Sees Afar, which Deganawidah placed on the very summit of the Tree, signified watchfulness. 'And the meaning of placing the Eagle on the top of the Tree,' said Deganawidah, 'is to watch the Roots which extend to the North and to the South and to the East and to the West, and the Eagle will discover if any evil is approaching your Confederacy, and will scream and give the alarm and come to the front.'

"'The Eagle,' said Deganawidah, 'shall have your power.' It was a reminder to his people that the best political contrivance that the wit of man can devise is impotent to keep the peace unless a watchful people stands always on guard to defend it.

"Then Deganawidah uprooted the Tree, and under it disclosed a Cavern through which ran a stream of water, passing out of sight into unknown regions under the earth. Into this current he cast the weapons of war, the hatchets and war-clubs, saying, 'We here rid the earth of these things of an Evil Mind.'

"Then, replacing the Tree, 'Thus,' he said, 'shall the Great Peace be established, and hostilities shall no longer be known between the Five Nations, but peace to the United People.'"

EXHORTATIONS OF AN AZTEC FATHER
TO HIS SON

"Endeavor to live an upright life," says Biart, in his book, *The Aztecs*, "ceaselessly praying God to help thee. He created thee, and to him thou belongest. He is thy father, and he loves thee even more than I love thee. Let thy thoughts be of him and address thy sighs to him night and day.

"Revere and salute thy elders, and never show them any sign of contempt. Be not silent to the poor and the unfortunate; but make haste to console them with kind words. Honor every one, but especially thy father and thy mother, to whom thou owest obedience, fear and service. Take care not to imitate the example of those bad sons who, like brutes devoid of reason, do not respect those who have given them life; who do not listen to their advice, and do not wish to submit to the punishment their elders judge necessary. He who follows the path of these evil-doers will come to a bad end; he will die in despair, thrown into an abyss, or by the claws of wild beasts.

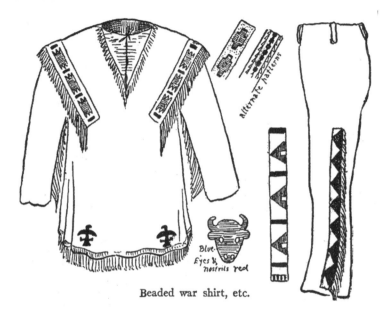

Beaded war shirt, etc.

"Never mock at old men, nor at deformed people. Do not mock him whom thou seest commit a fault, and do not throw it in his face. Enter into thyself, and fear lest that which offends thee in others may happen to thyself.

"Go not whither no one calls thee, and mix not thyself with what does not concern thee. By thy words, as well as by thy deeds, endeavor to prove thy good education. When thou talkest with any one, do not take hold of his garments. Do not talk too much, and never interrupt others with thy discourse. If thou hearest any one speak foolishly, if thou art not charged with his conduct, hold thy tongue. If thou shouldst not be silent, weigh thy words, and do not expose the fault with arrogance, lest thy lesson be not well received.

Quill worked war shirt

"When some one speaks to thee, hear him with attention and respect, without moving thy feet, without biting thy cloak, without spitting, and without getting up every minute if thou art seated; for these actions are signs of levity and of a bad education.

"When thou art at table, eat not too fast, and show no dislike if a dish displeases thee. If a person arrives at thy meal-time, divide thy meal with him and do not watch him as he eats.

"When thou walkest, look whither thou goest, that thou mayest knock against no one. If thou meetest any one in thy way, make room for him. Never pass before thy elders, unless forced by necessity, or unless they order thee to do so. When thou takest thy meal in their company, drink not before they do, and offer them what they need in order to gain their good will.

"If thou art made a present, accept it with gratitude. If the gift is of much value, be not proud of it, and if it be of small value, do not despise it nor mock at it; fear to wound him who wished to oblige thee.

"It thou growest rich, become not insolent to the poor, and humble them not; for the gods who have refused them wealth to give it to thee, might grow angry and take it from thee to favor another therewith. Live by thy work, for thou shalt be only the more happy therefore....

"Never lie, for it is a great sin. When thou tellest any one what has been told thee, tell the simple truth, and add nothing thereto. Slander no one, and be silent in regard to the faults thou seest in others, if it is not thy duty to correct them. When thou takest a message, if the one who receives it flies into a passion and speaks ill of the person who sent it, in repeating his words, modify their severity, in order that thou mayst not be the cause of a quarrel, nor of a scandal for which thou wouldst have to reproach thyself...."

LOVE FOR COUNTRY

There was no stronger impulse in the Indian than the deep abiding love of his country and the soil on which he and his people had lived for generations. Their most desperate fights were those in which the bravest gladly gave their lives to hold their own country for their own people.

"The honor of their tribe, and the welfare of their nation is the first and most predominant emotion of their hearts; and from hence proceed in a great measure all their virtues and their vices. Actuated by this, they brave every danger, endure the most exquisite torments, and expire triumphing in their fortitude, not as a personal qualification, but as a national characteristic."[37]

Sept. 17, 1912, I was sitting in Curley's lodge among the Crow Indians in Montana. He had been Custer's Chief Scout, and was the only survivor in Custer's last fight except White Swan, who barely lived through it. Curley was talking bitterly of the government's ingratitude in attempting to push his people off their ancient lands. He refused to sign the agreement and gave me a signed copy of his refusal on that occasion. It reads thus: "I was the friend of General Custer.

"I was one of his scouts and will say a few words.

"The Great Father in Washington sent you here about this land.

---

[37] Jonathan Carver, *Travels*, p. 271.

"The soil you see is not ordinary soil—it is the dust of the blood, the flesh and the bones of our ancestors.

"We fought and bled and died to keep other Indians from taking it, and we fought and bled and died helping the Whites.

"You will have to dig down through the surface before you can find nature's earth, as the upper portion is Crow.

"The land as it is, is my blood and my dead; it is consecrated; and I do not want to give up any portion of it."

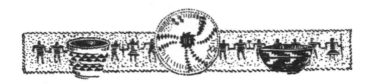

V

WABASHA

THE TEACHINGS OF WABASHA

(Also ascribed to Tecumseh, Sitting Bull, Crazy Horse, and Wovoka)

So live your life that the fear of death can never enter your heart.[1]

When you arise in the morning, give thanks for the morning light. Give thanks for your life and strength. Give thanks for your food and give thanks for the joy of living. And if perchance you see no reason for giving thanks, rest assured the fault is in yourself.[2]

Thank the Great Spirit for each meal; cast a morsel of meat into the fire and pray, "Great Spirit, partake with us."

Sin is trespass against the laws of the Great Spirit; it brings its own punishment, for sin *is* its own punishment. Crime is trespass against the laws of the tribe; and may be punished by the tribe.

No man shall suffer for the sin of another. No man can take the punishment of another, and so make the sinner guiltless.

---

[1] "The Whiteman's creed is the fear of dying; the Indian's creed is the joy of living."—Indian comment.

[2] J. J. Mathews says this was always chanted as an orison among his people, the Osages.

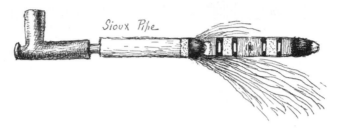

Sioux Pipe

It is unjust that a wicked man should escape the punishment of his crime. It is tenfold more unjust that an innocent man be punished in his place. God is not a hungry wild beast, demanding only a victim, it matters not who or what, so He be fed. Therefore, beware of the liars, that offer to secure for you an innocent, to bear the penalty of your sin, while you go free.

Be merciful to those who are in your power. It is the part of a coward to torture a prisoner or ill-treat those that are helpless before you. It is the part of a Chief to take care of the weak, the sick, the old and the helpless.

Only a coward ends his life by suicide; a brave man dies fighting.

Every village should have its Holy Place, its Medicine Lodge, where men may meet to dance the dance, smoke the good smoke, make medicine.

And every man should have his own Holy Place where he keeps lonely vigil, harkens for the Voices, and offers prayer and praise.

If by training, and a right life, and the gift of the Great Spirit, you have made your body beautiful, it is well to have your beauty seen by all, for an example and to give them pleasure. The veil of shame is well for those who are diseased or misshapen or unclean, and so made ugly.

If a wild beast attack your child, your wife, your house, your friend, or yourself, it is your duty as a man to fight with all your strength and with whatever weapons be at hand, and to destroy it as soon as possible or drive it off; and it is none the less your duty if that beast be in the form of a man.

Show respect to all men, but grovel to none.

It is more honorable to give than to receive.

Pray that the smell of your own people be a pleasant smell to you.

I have seen many men whose religion, judging by their lives, is the "love of money and the fear of death." But these were not Red men of the old faith.[3]

Do not speak of the dead except to recall their good deeds.

Do not speak to your mother-in-law at any time, or allow her to talk to you. If she be in the lodge when the son-in-law enters, she should drop her eyes, and leave in silence. This is the wisdom of the Ancients.

When you arrive at a strange camp or village, first pay your respects to the Chief before you call on your friends or acquaintances of lesser rank. It may be the Chief does not wish you to be received at all.

When you leave camp in the morning, clean up all your rubbish, burn or bury it. Do not go about polluting the land or destroying its beauty.

Do not stare at strangers; drop your eyes if they stare hard at you; and this, above all, for women.

Always give a word or sign of salute when meeting or passing a friend, or even a stranger, if in a lonely place.

A man is bound by his promise with a bond that cannot be broken except by permission of the other

---

[3] We are taught that the love of money is the root of all evil. If this be true, then was the Indian saved from much, for money was unknown among his tribes till brought by the Whiteman. Carver says that to the love of money the Indians "attribute all the mischiefs that are prevalent among the Europeans, such as treachery, plundering, devastation and murder" (*Travels*, p. 158); therefore, would none of it.

party. If that promise is on paper, that is merely to prove that he did give his word. It is not therefore more or less binding.

A Minisino (a man tried and proven) is at all times clean, courteous and master of himself.

If a man be given over to sex appetite, he is harboring a rattlesnake, whose sting is rottenness and sure death.

LAWS OF THE LODGE

Be hospitable. Be kind. Always assume that your guest is tired, cold, and hungry. If even a hungry dog enter your lodge, you must feed him.

Always give your guest the place of honor in the lodge, and at the feast, and serve him in reasonable ways. Never sit while your guest stands.

Go hungry rather than stint your guest. If he refuses certain food, say nothing; he may be under vow.

Protect your guest as one of the family; feed his horse, and beat your dogs if they harm his dog.

Do not trouble your guest with many questions about himself; he will tell you what he wishes you to know.[4]

---

[4] Oskenonton said that his father taught him: Do not even ask him his name. He may be a fugitive from justice, and that is none of your affair.

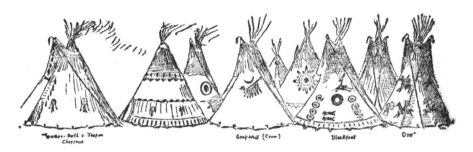

In another man's lodge, follow his customs, not your own.

Never worry your host with your troubles.

Always repay calls of courtesy; do not delay.

Give your host a little present on leaving; little presents are little courtesies and never give offence.

Say "Thank you" for every gift, however small.

Compliment your host, even if you must strain the facts to do so.

Never come between anyone and the fire.

Never walk between persons talking. Never interrupt persons talking.

In council, listen attentively to the other man's words as though they were words of wisdom, however much they may be otherwise.

Let not the young speak among those much older, unless asked.

When you address the council, carry a green bough in your hand, that yours may be living words.

Always give place to your seniors in entering or leaving the lodge. Never sit while your seniors stand.

Never force your conversation on anyone.

Let silence be your motto till duty bids you speak. Speak softly, especially before your elders or in presence of strangers.

Do not touch live coals with a steel knife or any sharp steel.

Do not break a marrow bone in the lodge; it is unlucky.

The women of the lodge are the keepers of the fire, but the men should help with the heavier sticks.

When setting up the tepees, keep the camp circle with its opening to the east, the door of each tepee to the sunrise.

Let each tepee be in its place, as long ago appointed by the old men—the wise ones—the nigh kin near each other, and the clans of different totems facing across the circle. In this wise the young men shall see that they must marry across the circle of the camp, never with their close kin in the nearer lodges.

Blackfoot

VI

THE WISDOM OF THE OLD MEN

IN THE BEGINNING

In the beginning, the Great Spirit made this world for His pleasure. He piled up the mountains, scooped out the lakes, traced the rivers, planted the forests; and to dwell in them, He created the insects, the fish, the reptiles, the birds, the beasts, and man—all of one flesh, and in all the breath of life, which is a measure of the Great Spirit.

All are His children—and man is but a little higher than the animals—he is better only in having a larger measure of understanding, and in better knowledge of the Great Spirit. So also in better gift, he has the power of hearing the Voices from which comes knowledge of the Unseen World.

GENESIS

From the ritual of the Omaha Pebble Society:[1] "At the beginning, all things were in the mind of Wakonda. All creatures, including man, were spirits. They moved about in space between the earth and the stars (the heavens). They were seeking a place where they could

---

[1] Fletcher-La Flesche, *27th Ann. Rep. Bur. Eth.*, 1911, p. 570.

come into a bodily existence. They ascended to the sun, but the sun was not fitted for their abode. They moved on to the moon and found that it also was not good for their home. Then they descended to the earth. They saw it was covered with water. They floated through the air to the north, the east, the south, and the west, and found no dry land. They were sorely grieved. Suddenly from the midst of the water uprose a great rock. It burst into flames, and the waters floated into the air in clouds. Dry land appeared; the grasses and the trees grew. The hosts of spirits descended and became flesh and blood. They fed on the seeds of the grasses and the fruits of the trees, and the land vibrated with their expressions of joy and gratitude to Wakonda, the maker of all things."

THE QUICHÉ'S MYTH OF CREATION[2]

"This is the first word and the first speech: There were neither man nor brutes, neither birds, fish nor crabs, stick nor stone, valley nor mountain, stubble nor forest, nothing but the sky.

"The face of the land was hidden; there was naught but the silent sea and the sky.

"There was nothing joined, nor any sound, nor thing that stirred; neither any to do evil, nor to rumble in the heavens, nor a walker on foot; only the silent waters, only the pacified ocean, only it in its calm.

"Nothing was, but stillness and rest and darkness and the night.

"Nothing but the Maker and Molder, the Hurler, the Bird Serpent.

"In the waters, in a limpid twilight, covered with green feathers, slept the mothers and the fathers.

---

[2] From Ximenez' *Myths of the Quiché Indians.*

"And over all passed Hurakan, the night wind, the black rushing Raven, and cried with rumbling croak, 'Earth! Earth!' and straightway the solid land was there."

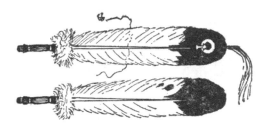

CLEAN FATHERHOOD[3]

"This is the sum of everything that is noble and honorable—Clean Fatherhood"—the words of Chief Capilano of the Squamish.

OMAHA PROVERBS[4]

"Stolen food never satisfies hunger."
"A poor man is a hard rider."
"All persons dislike a borrower."
"No one mourns the thriftless."
"The path of the lazy leads to disgrace."
"A man must make his own arrows."
"A handsome face does not make a good husband."

---

[3] Tekahionwake (Emily Pauline Johnson), *Legends of Vancouver*, 1912, p. 10.
[4] Fletcher-La Flesche, *27th Ann. Rep. Bur. Eth.*, 1911, p. 604.

SAYINGS OF THE ANCIENTS[5]

"Never go to sleep when your meat is on the fire."
(Blackfeet)

"Would you choose a counselor, watch him with
his neighbor's children." (Sioux)

"If a skunk walk on your trail and leave a stink
there, do not go out of your way to prove that it is not
your stink." (Paiute)

"If the poor be poor in spirit as well as in appear-
ance, how shall they be aught but poor to the end of
their days?" (Zuni)

"The moon is not disturbed by the barking of
dogs." (Southwest)

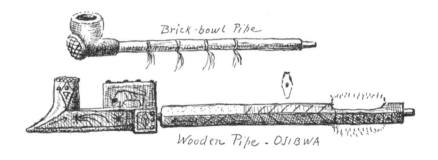

Brick-bowl Pipe

Wooden Pipe - OJIBWA

TO THE DEAD DEER

"I am sorry I had to kill thee, Little Brother.
But I had need of thy meat.
My children were hungry and crying for food.
Forgive me, Little Brother.

---

[5] From Mary Austin, *One Smoke Stories*, 1934, by permission of Hough-
ton Mifflin Co.

I will do honor to thy courage, thy strength and thy
  beauty.
See, I will hang thine horns on this tree.
I will decorate them with red streamers.
Each time I pass, I will remember thee and do honor
  to thy spirit.
I am sorry I had to kill thee.
Forgive me, Little Brother.
See, I smoke to thy memory.
I burn tobacco."

THE OLD ONION SELLER

In a shady corner of the great market at Mexico City was
an old Indian named Pota-lamo. He had twenty strings
of onions hanging in front of him.

An American from Chicago came up and said:
"How much for a string of onions?"

"Ten cents," said Pota-lamo.

"How much for two strings?"

"Twenty cents," was the reply.

"How much for three strings?"

"Thirty cents," was the answer.

"Not much reduction in that," said the American.
"Would you take twenty-five cents?"

"No," said the Indian.

"How much for your whole twenty strings?" said the
American.

"I would not sell you my twenty strings," replied the
Indian.

"Why not?" said the American. "Aren't you here to
sell your onions?"

"No," replied the Indian. "I am here to live my life.
I love this market place. I love the crowds and the red
serapes. I love the sunlight and the waving palmettos. I

love to have Pedro and Luis come by and say: 'Buenos días,' and light cigarettes and talk about the babies and the crops. I love to see my friends. That is my life. For that I sit here all day and sell my twenty strings of onions. But if I sell all my onions to one customer, then is my day ended. I have lost my life that I love—and that I will not do."

THE LESSONS OF LONE-CHIEF, SKUR-AR-ALE-SHAR, GIVEN HIM BY HIS WIDOWED MOTHER[6]

"When you get to be a man, remember that it is ambition that makes the man.

"If you go on the warpath, do not turn around when you have gone part way, but go on as far as you were going; then come back.

"If I should live to see you become a man, I want you to become a great man. I want you to think about the hard times we have been through.

"Take pity on people who are poor, because we have been poor, and people have taken pity on us.

[6] George Bird Grinnell, *Pawnee Hero Stories and Folk Tales*, 1892, pp. 46-7.

"If I live to see you a man, and to go off on the warpath, I would not cry if I were to hear that you had been killed in battle. That is what makes a man, to fight and to be brave.

"Love your friend and never desert him. If you see him surrounded by the enemy do not run away; go to him, and if you cannot save him, be killed together and let your bones lie side by side."

TECUMSEH'S SPEECH[7]

(From the speech of Tecumseh to Governor Harrison at Vincennes, August 12, 1810, repudiating a fraudulent purchase of his people's hunting grounds by the American government.)

"I am a Shawnee. My forefathers were warriors. Their son is a warrior. From them I take only my existence, from my Tribe I take nothing. I am the maker of my own fortune, and Oh! that I could make that of my Red people, and of my country, as great as the conceptions of my mind, when I think of the Spirit that rules the universe. I would not then come to Governor Harrison to ask him to tear up the treaty, and to obliterate the landmark, but I would say to him: 'Sir, you have liberty to return to your own country.'

"The Being within, communing with past ages, tells me that once, nor until lately, there was no Whiteman on this continent, that it then all belonged to the Redman, children of the same parents, placed on it by the Great Spirit that made them, to keep it, to traverse it, to enjoy its productions, and to fill it with the same

---

[7] From Sam G. Drake's *Book of the Indians*, 1836, Book V, Chapter VII, p. 121.

race, once a happy race; since made miserable by the White people, who are never contented but always encroaching.

"The way, and the only way to check and to stop this evil, is for all the Red men to unite, in claiming a common and equal right in the land, as it was at first and should be yet; for it was never divided, but belongs to all for the use of each. That no part has a right to sell, even to each other, much less to strangers—those who want all and will not do with less. The White people have no right to take the land from the Indians, because they had it first, it is theirs. They may sell, but all must join. Any sale not made by all, is not valid. The late sale is bad. It was made by a part only. Part do not know how to sell. It requires all to make a bargain for all. All Red men have equal rights to the unoccupied land. The right to occupancy is as good in one place as in another. There cannot be two occupations in the same place. The first excludes all others. It is not so in hunting or traveling, for there the same ground will serve many, as they may follow each other all day, but the camp is stationary, and that is occupancy. It belongs to the first who sits down on his blanket or skins, which he has thrown upon the ground, and till he leaves it, no other has a right."

RED JACKET'S REPLY TO MISSIONARY CRAM AT BUFFALO, N.Y., 1805[8]

After the missionary had done speaking, the Indians conferred together about two hours, by themselves, when they gave an answer by Red Jacket, which follows: "Friend and brother, it was the will of the Great Spirit that we should meet together this day. He orders all

[8] From Sam G. Drake's *Book of the Indians*, Book V, pp. 98-100.

DECORATION OF BLACK BULL'S TEEPEE: (TWO EXAMPLES OF DOORS)

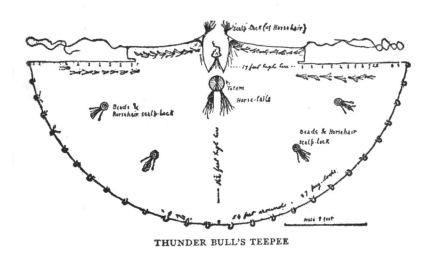

THUNDER BULL'S TEEPEE

things, and He has given us a fine day for our council. He has taken His garment from before the sun, and caused it to shine with brightness upon us; our eyes are opened, that we see clearly; our ears are unstopped, that we have been able to hear distinctly the words that

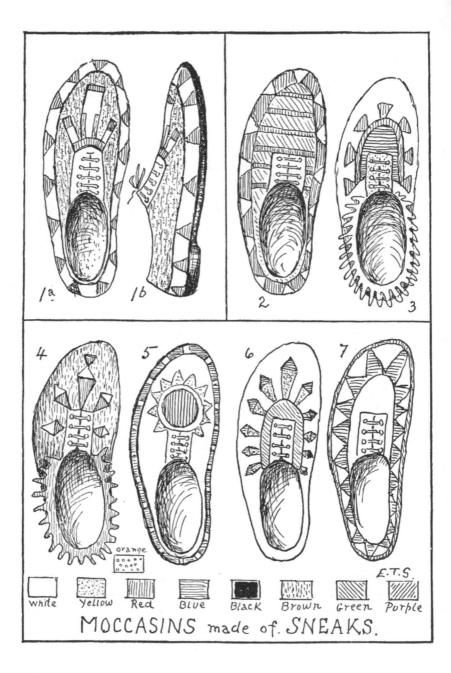

1a   1b   2   3

4   5   6   7

orange

É.T.S.

white   Yellow   Red   Blue   Black   Brown   Green   Purple

MOCCASINS made of SNEAKS.

you have spoken; for all these favors we thank the Great Spirit, and Him only.

"Brother, this council fire was kindled by you; it was at your request that we came together at this time; we have listened with attention to what you have said; you requested us to speak our minds freely; this gives us great joy, for we now consider that we stand upright before you, and can speak what we think; all have heard your voice, and all speak to you as one man; our minds are agreed.

"Brother, you say you want an answer to your talk, before you leave this place. It is right you should have one, as you are a great distance from home, and we do not wish to detain you; but we will first look back a little, and tell you what our fathers have told us, and what we have heard from the White people.

"Brother, listen to what we say. There was a time when our forefathers owned this great land. Their seats extended from the rising to the setting sun. The Great Spirit had made it for the use of Indians. He had created the buffalo, the deer, and other animals for food. He made the bear and the beaver, and their skins served us for clothing. He had scattered them over the country, and taught us how to take them. He had caused the earth to produce corn for bread.

"All this He had done for His Red children because He loved them. If we had any disputes about hunting grounds, they were generally settled without the shedding of much blood.

"But an evil day came upon us; your forefathers crossed the great waters, and landed on this island. Their numbers were small; they found friends, and not enemies; they told us they had fled from their own country for fear of wicked men, and come here to enjoy their religion. They asked for a small seat; we took pity on them, granted their request, and they sat down amongst us; we gave them corn and meat; they gave us poison in return. [Spirituous liquor is alluded to, it is supposed.] The White people had now found our country, tidings were carried back, and more came amongst us; yet we did not fear them, we took them to be friends; they called us brothers; we believed them, and gave them a larger seat. At length their numbers had greatly increased; they wanted more land; they wanted our country. Our eyes were opened; and our minds became uneasy. Wars took place; Indians were hired to fight against Indians, and many of our people were destroyed. They also brought strong liquors among us; it was strong and powerful, and has slain thousands.

"Brother, our seats were once large, and yours were very small; you have now become a great people, and we have scarcely a place left to spread our blankets; you have got our country, but are not satisfied; you want to force your religion upon us.

"Brother, continue to listen. You say that you are sent to instruct us how to worship the Great Spirit agreeably to His mind, and if we do not take hold of the religion which you White people teach, we shall be unhappy hereafter; you say that you are right, and we are lost; how do we know this to be true? We understand that your religion is written in a book; if it was intended for us as well as you, why has not the Great Spirit given it to us, and not only to us, but why did He not give to our forefathers the knowledge of that book, with the means of understanding it rightly? We only know what you tell us about it; how shall we know when to believe, being so often deceived by the White people?

"Brother, you say there is but one way to worship and serve the Great Spirit; if there is but one religion, why do you White people differ so much about it? Why not all agree, as you can all read the book?

"Brother, we do not understand these things; we are told that your religion was given to your forefathers, and has been handed down from father to son. We also have a religion which was given to our forefathers, and has been handed down to us, their children. We worship that way. It teaches us to be thankful for all the favors we receive; to love each other, and to be united; we never quarrel about religion.

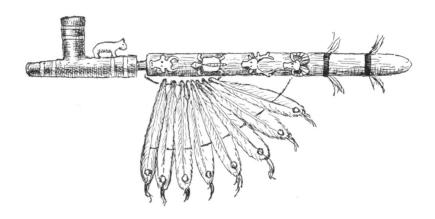

"Brother, the Great Spirit has made us all; but He has made a great difference between His White and Red children; He has given us a different complexion and different customs; to you He has given the arts; to these He has not opened our eyes; we know these things to be true. Since He has made so great a difference between us in other things, why may we not conclude that He has given us a different religion according to our understanding? The Great Spirit does right; He knows what is best for His children; we are satisfied.

"Brother, we do not wish to destroy your religion, or take it from you. We want only to enjoy our own.

"Brother, you say you have not come to get our land or our money, but to enlighten our minds. I will now tell you that I have been at your meetings, and saw you collecting money from the meeting. I cannot tell what this money was intended for, but suppose it was for your minister, and if we should conform to your way of thinking, perhaps you may want some from us.

"Brother, we are told that you have been preaching to White people in this place; these people are our neighbors, we are acquainted with them; we will wait a

Bull Calf's Teehee

little while and see what effect your preaching has upon them. If we find it does them good, makes them honest, and less disposed to cheat Indians, we will then consider again what you have said.

"Brother, you have now heard our answer to your talk, and this is all we have to say at present. As we are going to part, we will come and take you by the hand, and hope the Great Spirit will protect you on your journey, and return you safe to your friends."

The chiefs and others then drew near the missionary to take him by the hand; but he would not receive them, and hastily rising from his seat, said, that "there was no fellowship between the religion of God and the works of the Devil, and, therefore, could not join hands with them." Upon this being interpreted to them, "they smiled, and retired in a peaceable manner."

SITTING BULL'S APPEAL TO THE INDIAN AGENT[9]

"All the Indians pray to God for life, and try to find out a good road, and do nothing wrong in this life. This is what we want, and to pray to God. But you did not believe us.

"You should say nothing against our religion, for we say nothing against yours. You pray to God. So do all of us Indians, as well as the Whites. We both pray to only one God, who made us all."

THE DEATH OF NOCONA[10]

The Texan Rangers had been organized to drive the Comanches from their ancient hunting grounds along the Pease River. A company of these hard, two-fisted, straight-shooting veterans, eighty in number, under

---

[9] Stanley Vestal, *Sitting Bull*, 1932, p. 291.

[10] By special permission from *The Gentlemen in the White Hats*, by C. L. Douglas, pp. 63-65, Turner Company, Dallas, Texas, 1934.

Captain Sul Ross, were joined by twenty men of the Second United States Cavalry, and set out to find the Indian camp on Pease River, December 18, 1860.

They reached the Comanche village at sunrise during a sand storm. The inhabitants, chiefly women and children and a handful of warriors armed with bows and arrows, were not yet aroused for the day. So the Rangers had no difficulty in surrounding the village before their presence was known.

Then the Chief Ranger shouted the order for attack.

"In less time than it takes in the telling, they were in among the tipis, hacking, hewing, and using the pistol with deadly, close-range accuracy. The warriors fought with valor, attempting as best they could to hold up the attackers until their women and children could make a getaway on the fleet Indian ponies, many of which already had been nose-looped for a morning buffalo hunt. And in a measure they succeeded. Many of the squaws, and even some of the braves, were fortunate enough to find mounts—but they galloped into the waiting arms of the cavalry dragoons.

"The fight was over before it fairly started....

"Chief Peta Nocona himself was lucky enough to gain a pony's back; and pulling a fifteen-year-old girl up behind him, he darted northward in an effort to dodge the cavalrymen. Trailing him, on another fast mustang, rode a squaw, an infant in her arms....

"Nocona rode like a wind-blown devil, both arms of the girl encircling his waist....

"The squaw, clutching the baby to her breast, rode with the buckskin rein free, beating with her heels a steady tattoo on the horse's ribs. A true Centaur of the Plains, this woman of the Comanche, and even Kelleher admired her.

"'Take the squaw…capture her!' shouted Captain Ross. 'I'll go after the Chief!'

"Ross steadily gained ground, edging ahead of the lieutenant, and finally passed the fleeing woman. He glanced back only once—to see Kelleher grasp the nose strap of the squaw's pony and pull in the fugitives. Then he turned his sole attention to Peta Nocona.

"The Chief's horse, weighted as it was, was tiring fast—and now Sul Ross was galloping only twenty yards behind. The captain drew a pistol from his belt, raised it and swung down from the shoulder.

"Crack!…The girl swayed, clutched once at Nocona's girdle, and toppled from the plunging horse, drilled neatly through the back. But she had caught the girdle, and it was tight about the chieftain's waist; she pulled Nocona with her as she fell.

"But Nocona, catlike, had landed on his feet, and in the flash of a second had whipped the bow from over his shoulders and had strung an arrow with that great speed which only the Plains Indian can display. Thus Ross, before he could swerve aside, was made target for two long-shafted arrows, the point of one embedding itself in the left shoulder of his charger.

"The captain's horse, stabbed with pain, went wild, but Ross sawed on the bridle, quieted him somewhat and circled back to finish off Nocona. He found the Chief standing where he had left him, beside the dying girl, an arrow strung and ready. He loosed it as the Ranger galloped back to renew the attack, but the shaft went wide; and Ross, clinging to the pommel of his saddle with the left hand, let go another pistol shot. The ball struck Nocona in the right arm, breaking the bone.

"'Then,' said Captain Ross, telling the story later, 'I shot the Chief twice through the body, whereupon he deliberately walked to a small tree, and leaning against it, began to sing a wild, weird song.'

"Ross dismounted and walked toward the Chief.

"'Surrender?' he called, but Nocona shook his head, brandishing in one last defiant gesture the lance he held in his left hand.

"A Mexican member of the Ranger company rode up and dismounted; he carried in the crook of his arm a long-barreled shotgun.

"'Finish him!' ordered Captain Ross.

"The Mexican raised the shotgun and pulled the trigger.

"Nocona, still singing his wild, weird song—the Death Chant of the Comanche—stood straight as a lance... proud... erect... defiant.

"And then he fell—an arrow in the dust."

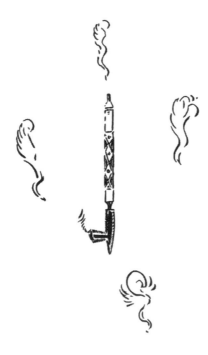

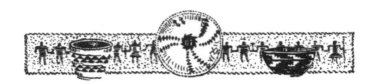

VII

PROPHETS OF THE RED RACE

HIAWATHA, the great prophet of the Iroquois Con-
federation. He was a Mohawk of the Tortoise Clan—and
probably lived about A.D. 1570. He recognized the fact
that internal dissension and petty feuds were the greatest of the evils that preyed on the Redmen, and therefore founded the Iroquois League, a league of nations
that aimed at general peace and well-being, substituting
a tribunal of justice to settle internal disputes in place of
the arbitrament of war.

Longfellow's poem, "Hiawatha," founded on
Henry Rowe Schoolcraft's version of the Hiawatha tradition in *Algic Researches,* is in its main outline believed to
be historically correct.

POWHATAN (1547-1618), the Head Chief and
founder of the Powhatan Confederacy of Virginia. At
first he was friendly toward the White invaders; but, em-
bittered by their treachery and robberies, he declared
open war. Pocahontas was his daughter.

METACOMET, born 1620 (?), died August 12, 1676,
also known as King Philip, Sachem of the Wampanoag.
The most remarkable of the Indians of New England.
Realizing that the Whites were planning to possess the
whole country, to which end they proposed to extermi-
nate the Indians, he made preparation for nine years;
and, in 1675, declared war against the invaders. After

taking and destroying twelve White towns he was slain while leading his warriors in an attack on Mount Hope, Rhode Island, August 12, 1676.

WABASHA, a Santee Sioux, born 1718 on the Rum River, Minnesota. He was a great chief and warrior as well as a philosopher of practical common sense, one of the best exponents of the Indian philosophy. He died in 1799. His son, grandson, and great-grandson all bore the name of Wabasha or Wapasha.

PONTIAC, the Great Ottawa Chief, born on the Maumee River, Ohio, 1720. He planned a grand federation of all Indian tribes to drive back the Whitemen and confirm the Indians in their ancient possessions. His armies successfully attacked Sandusky, St. Joseph, Miami, Quiatenon, Michilimackinac, Presqu' Isle, Le Boeuf, and Venango, but were repulsed at Detroit and Fort Pitt.

These defeats, combined with the fact that his allies, the French, had made peace with Great Britain, forced him to make terms with the Whites, signing a treaty of peace at Detroit, August 17, 1765. Four years afterwards he was murdered by a drunken Indian at Cahokia, Illinois.

Pontiac stands next to Tecumseh as a great leader of the Red men.

TECUMSEH, the Great Shawnee Chief, born at Piqua, Ohio, 1768, died in battle at Thamesville, Ontario, October 5, 1813, in his forty-fifth year.[1]

He was doubtless the greatest of all the American Indians, the one character in American history of whom it may be said, he was a great warrior, a great statesman, a great hunter, a great athlete, and a great leader, a man whose life was without weakness or blemish. According to the record, he represented the noblest type of manhood produced in the Western World, no matter what race be considered.

He denied the right of any small Tribe to dispose of lands that were obviously held by all the Tribes, and for this reason denounced all treaties recently made with the United States.

Tecumseh realized that nothing could stop the destructive march of the invading White race but a federation of all the Indian Tribes, and devoted his whole life and energies to the foundation of such a league of the people.

He it was who, for humane reasons, put a stop to torture of prisoners by the English soldiers as well as by Indians, although it was the custom in all armies of the time, especially those of Europe.

BLACK HAWK, a Chief and distinguished warrior in the Sauk and Fox Tribe. Born on the Rock River, Illinois,

---

[1] After narrating the death of Tecumseh at the battle of Thamesville, Drake, the historian, adds: "That the American soldiers should have dishonored themselves after their victory, by outraging all decency by acts of astonishing ferocity and barbarity upon the lifeless body of the fallen Chief, is grievous to mention, and cannot meet with too severe condemnation. Pieces of his skin were taken away by some of them as mementoes.

"We have often heard it said but whether in truth we do not aver, that there are those who still own razor straps made of it" (Sam G. Drake, *Book of the Indians*, 1836, Book V, Chap. VII, p. 125).

1767; died, October 3, 1838. He was the leader of his people in the Black Hawk War of 1832. His most famous exploit was the total defeat of an army of 270 Kentucky riflemen who, under Major Stillman, were sent against him. He met them with 40 warriors, and inflicted a humiliating defeat, killing and wounding many. The survivors fled for thirty miles—"some never stopped till they were safe at home."[2]

SEQUOYA. Born in Taskigi, Tennessee, about 1760, died near San Fernando, Tamaulipas, Mexico, August, 1845. He was the son of a Whiteman and a Cherokee woman of mixed blood. In 1821 he invented and perfected a syllabic alphabet of eighty-five characters so rational and simple that after a few months thousands of his people learned it and were thus enabled to read and write their own language.

CRAZY HORSE, a famous Chief of the Oglala Sioux. His teachings were full of inspiration and on the highest plane of ethics.

Crazy Horse was next in command to Sitting Bull at the Custer fight. After surrendering under guarantee of protection, Crazy Horse was assassinated by Government agents, September 7, 1877.

SITTING BULL, the famous Chief of the Hunkpapa Sioux, was born on the Grand River of South Dakota, March 1831, and was deliberately murdered by agents of the Government at Standing Rock, December 15, 1890.

[2] N. B. Wood, *Lives of Famous Indian Chiefs*, 1906, p. 367.

Although a war chief and an organizer, he was also a dreamer, a mystic, a clairvoyant, and a philosopher of deep natural insight.

He was the greatest Indian of his time, and so influential that the Indian Bureau determined to get rid of him by any means at hand.

His clairvoyant powers notified him of Custer's approach on June 24, 1876, with a great army determined to destroy him and his people with all the women and children. The grandeur of his soul is evidenced in his appeal to God Almighty, for his concern was not for himself but for his people. The night before the fight, he left camp and, climbing to the top of a near hill, he prayed.

"Standing on that hilltop so soon to be made bloody in the fight which 'Long Hair' was seeking, the Chief raised his hands to the dark sky, and wailed and prayed to God who had promised him the victory: 'Wakan Tanka, pity me. In the name of the nation, I offer You this pipe. Wherever the Sun, Moon, Earth, Four Winds there You are always. Father, save these people, I beg You. *We wish to live!* Guard us against all misfortunes and calamities. Take pity.'

"Sitting Bull went home then. He left up there small offerings of tobacco tied to wands stuck in the ground. Next day the hooves of Custer's troop horses knocked them down. But, the Sioux say, those offerings were not in vain."[3]

SMOHALLA, a great prophet and teacher of the Nez Percé or Sahaptin tribe. He urged the Indians to return to their primitive mode of life and to refuse the teachings of the Whiteman, to abstain from things sup-

[3] Stanley Vestal, *Sitting Bull,* p. 161.

plied by the Whiteman, especially the firewater, and to be guided in all ways by the will of God as revealed in dreams and through the prophets. He was born about 1817 and died about 1900.

GERONIMO or GOYATHLAY, a great Medicine Man and War Chief of the Chiricahua Apaches, was born about 1834 on the Gila River, New Mexico, near old Fort Tulerosa, and died at Fort Sill, Oklahoma, 1909. He and his people were driven to desperation by the continual encroachments of the Whites, by their total disregard of law and treaties when the interests of the Indians were at stake.

The war against Geronimo, 1885-6, was "one of the most remarkable in recorded history." In this 35 men, encumbered with women and children, with no supplies or ammunition except what they captured, maintained themselves for eighteen months against 5,000 regular troops and 500 Indian auxiliaries, besides border scouts in unknown and varying numbers, all with unlimited supplies. During this time, the Apaches killed a couple of hundred Whites and lost only six warriors, *not one of them killed by the soldiers.*[4]

WOVOKA, a Paiute Medicine Man, born in Nevada, 1856. He had a vision that Jesus Christ was coming again on earth to put an end to war, famine, and discord, and established the Ghost Dance or Spirit Dance in His honor. In his own briefest presentation it proclaimed, "You must not fight. Do no harm to anyone. Do right always."

"The Ghost Dance was entirely Christian," says Stanley Vestal, "except for the difference in rituals.

[4] Britton Davis, *The Truth About Geronimo*, 1929, p. xv.
[5] Stanley Vestal, *Sitting Bull*, p. 279.

Moreover it taught non-resistance and brotherly love in ways that had far more significance for Indians than any the missionaries could offer."[5]

Nevertheless, for taking part in this Dance, many hundreds of Indians—men, women and children—were brutally slaughtered by the American Government on December 29, 1890.

Stormcap.

Door.

Teepee with Stormcap.

Chipewyan Teepee
with Tent Bedroom.

E. T. Seton

VIII

WHITE EXPRESSIONS OF INDIAN THOUGHT

Many Whitemen and women have lived so close to the Redman that they have glimpsed something of his soul, and have been able to give it expression in words and word pictures that are nothing less than precious revelations to us.

As examples of these, I give the following:

HEARTS'S FRIEND[1]

by Mary Austin

Fair is the white star of twilight
And the sky clearer
At the day's end;
But she is fairer,
And she is dearer,
She, my heart's friend!

Fair is the white star of twilight
And the moon roving
To the sky's end;

---

[1] This and the following four poems by Mary Austin are reprinted from her book, *The American Rhythm*, 1923.

113

But she is fairer,
And she is dearer,
She, my heart's friend!

SONG FOR THE PASSING OF A BEAUTIFUL WOMAN

by Mary Austin

Strong sun across the sod can make
Such quickening as your countenance!
I am more worth for what your passing wakes,
Great races in my loins, to you that cry.
My blood is redder for your loveliness.

SONG FOR THE NEW BORN
(To be sung by the one who first takes the child from
its mother)

by Mary Austin

Newborn, on the naked sand
Nakedly lay it
Next to the earth mother,
That it may know her;
Having good thoughts of her, the food giver.
Newborn, we tenderly
In our arms take it,
Making good thoughts.
House-god, be entreatd,
That it may grow from childhood to manood,
Happy, contented;
Beautifully walking
The trail to old age.
Having good thoughts of the earth its mother,
That she may give it the fruits of her being.

Newborn, on the naked sand
Nakedly lay it.

PRAYER TO THE MOUNTAIN SPIRIT

by Mary Austin

Young man, Chieftain,
Reared within the mountain,
Lord of the Mountain,
Hear a young man's prayer!

Hear a prayer for cleanness,
Keeper of the *he* rain,
Drumming on the mountain,
Lord of the *she* rain
That restores the earth in newness;
Keeper of the clean rain,
Hear a prayer for wholeness!

Young man, Chieftain,
Hear a prayer for fleetness,
Keeper of the deer's way,
Reared among the eagles,
Clear my feet of slothness!
Keeper of the Paths of Men,
Hear a prayer for straightness!

Hear a prayer for courage!
Keeper of the lightning,
Reared amid the thunder,
Keeper of the dark cloud
At the doorway of the morning,
Hear a prayer for staunchness.
Young man, Chieftain,
Spirit of the Mountain!

LAMENT OF A MAN FOR HIS SON

by Mary Austin

Son, my son!
I will go up to the mountain
And there I will light a fire
To the feet of my son's spirit,
And there will I lament him;
Saying,
O my son,
What is my life to me, now you are departed!

Son, my son,
In the deep earth
We softly laid thee in a Chief's robe,
In a warrior's gear,
Surely there,
In the spirit land
Thy deeds attend thee!
Surely,
The corn comes to the ear again!

But I, here,
I am the stalk that the seed-gatherers
Descrying empty, afar, left standing.
Son, my son!
What is my life to me, now you are departed!

THE LAST SONG[2]

by Hartley Burr Alexander

Let it be beautiful
    when I sing the last song—
Let it be day!

I would stand upon my two feet,
    singing!
I would look upward with open yes,
    singing!

I would have the winds to envelop my body;
I would have the sun to shine upon my body;
The whole world I would have to make music with
    me.

Let it be beautiful
    when thou wouldst slay me, O Shining One!
Let it be day
    when I sing the last song!

[2] From *God's Drum,* 1927.

Chipewyan teepees with separate smoke flap

GOD'S DRUM

by Hartley Burr Alexander

The circle of the Earth is the head of a great drum;
With the day, it moves upward—booming;
With the night, it moves downward—booming;
The day and the night are its song.
I am very small, as I dance upon the drum-head;
I am like a particle of dust, as I dance upon the
    drum-head;
Above me in the sky is the shining ball of the drum
    stick.

I dance upward with the day;
I dance downward with the night;
Some day I shall dance afar into space like a
    particle of dust.

Who is the Drummer who beats upon the earth-
    drum?
Who is the Drummer who makes me to dance his
    song?

SHOES OF DEATH

by Lilian White Spencer

My brave goes on the warpath. At his belt
Hang wee worn moccasins.
Our child has others now, small but splendid
With gay beaded soles
Used only by walkers on air.
When he lay sick, I made them, weeping,
In haste yet beautifully:
I had not thought to fashion sandals of the grave

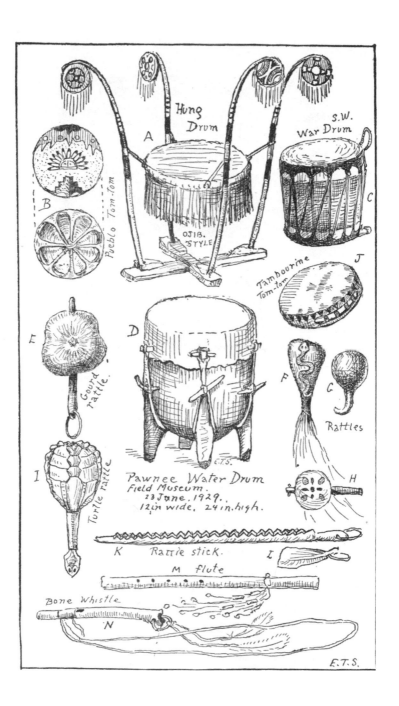

A Hung Drum

OJIB. STYLE

B Pueblo Tom-Tom

C S.W. War Drum

J Tambourine Tom-Tom

E Gourd rattle.

D Pawnee Water Drum
Field Museum.
23 June, 1929.
12 in wide. 24 in. high.

E.T.S.

F G Rattles

H

I Turtle rattle

K Rattle stick.

L

M flute

Bone Whistle

N

E.T.S.

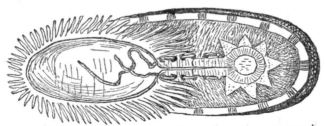

Moccasin, made of a rubber-soled shoe or sneak.
embroidery of silk, red, white, blue & yellow.
Around the ankle a fringe of leather.

Ojibwa Moccasin
with puckered front.

For one so young.
His father takes the little life-shoes
To bind on a slain enemy;
Thus, he will find our babe in the spirit-world
And be his friend.

The Omahas return singing.
My man has scalps at his side,
Not tiny moccasins that tread my heart.
His proud strength strides to us,
Sits by my side, smiling;
Smiling sinks to earth
Which reddens with his secret wound....

They draw white last lines on his face:
Two and two and two and two.
They speak: "You came with the holy Buffalo:
We wrap you in their sacred hide. Go back to them!
Turn no more this bitter way!
Be strong! Your four souls seek four heaven-winds."

I cut my hair above him. I gash my arms for sorrow.
My cries shall follow—follow....
Wailings are flute and drum-call to the dead.
See, on his happy feet
That will fly the trail of our son,
What I wrought with laughter
In our days of bridal,
Thinking to be quiet on my hilltop
Long, long before his need.
"Wokonda, God-Mystery, your warrior is ready!
His steps touch earth no more
Who wears splendid moccasins
With gay beaded soles."

THERE IS NO UNBELIEF

by Alfred Wooler

There is no unbelief!
Whoever plants a seed beneath the sod
And waits to see it push away the clod,
He trusts in God!
He trusts in God!

Whoever says when clouds are in the sky,
"Be patient, heart, light breaketh by and by,"
Trusts the Most High!
Trusts the Most High!

Whoever sees 'neath winter's field of snow
The silent harvest of the future grow,
God's pow'r must know!
God's pow'r must know!

Whoever lies upon his couch to sleep
Content to lock each sense in slumber deep,
Knows God will keep!
Knows God will keep!

There is no unbelief![3]

---

[3] These noble lines, though written by a Whiteman, are except in the matter of rhyme, wholly Indian in thought and form.

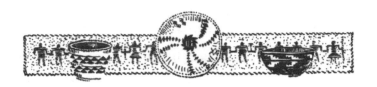

IX

WHITHER?

THE VISION

I had a vision for my people. I dreamed of a man who should be clean, manly, strong, unsordid, fearless and kind, gentle with his strength, dignified, silent and friendly, equipped for emergencies and filled with a religion that was built not of books or creeds or occasional observances, but of desire to help those that had need of help; not in the vague beyond of another world, but here among us—here—now—today.

I had my picture, and I sought him in the life and in the history near at hand, but found him not.

The life of pioneer and plainsman seemed to call with all insistence for such manhood and such men. And I was willing to believe. But, oh, the horror of their lives when I searched the record even as written by their friends. In full detail I saw with my own eyes and learned the lives of the backwoods types, the frontiersmen, the plainsmen, the scouts of the great Ohio woods. I found them, almost without exception, treacherous, murderous, worthless without the shadow of a claim on our respect but this: at best, a measure of dull brute grit that came in some sort from consciousness of their better weapons, of guns to match the arrow and the bow, and knowledge that, backing them, though far away, was an army of their kind, in overwhelming numbers coming on.

And still I held my vision of the perfect man,—athletic, fearless, kind, picturesque, wise in the ways of the woods, and without reproach of life. And by a long, long trail, with ample knowledge of histories and of persons, I was led, as many before have been, to choose the ideal American Indian. By all the evidence at hand, his was a better system, a better thought, because it produced far nobler, better men. He, more than any type I know, is the stuff that fires our highest dreams of manhood, realized complete. Him, therefore, I proclaim as the model for an outdoor life, our travel guide on the fourfold way that leads to perfect manhood.

My lifelong dream and hope is that I may be the instrument of giving to the Whiteman's world the inspiring teachings of the American Indian, in all and the full measure of their values.

EPILOGUE

THE REDMAN'S MESSAGE

The Civilization of the Whiteman is a failure; it is visibly crumbling around us. It has failed at every crucial test. No one who measures things by results can question this fundamental statement.

Apparently, the money-madness is the main cause of it all. We know that such a thing was unknown among the Indians. Their big menace was failure of food supply, and against this they prepared by a storage plan that was effectual.

What is Civilization? Literally, it is a system by which men can live in a large group (a city, or *civitas*) and enjoy all the benefits without suffering the evils that result from such association.

For example, a man with his family is living isolated in the woods. They make or capture all the necessaries of life. They defend themselves by fighting against the next family on the next stream, and their only answer to sanitary problems is to move out when the camp stinks.

But suppose one hundred families agree to live together in the same camp, and combine their efforts to solve more effectively the problems of hostile tribes, food failure, disease, social pleasures, spiritual life. The men become *cives*. The resultant system evolved is a *Civilization*.

How are we going to appraise the value of a Civilization? By certain yard measures that are founded on human nature, and which remorselessly investigate the fundamentals of the man-mind and the man-needs.

First of these is: Does your Civilization guarantee to you absolute freedom of action so long as you do not encroach on the equal right of your neighbor to do the same thing?

Does your system work for the greatest happiness of the greatest number?

Is your Civilization characterized by justice in the courts and gentleness in the streets?

Are its largest efforts to relieve suffering and misery?

Does your Civilization grant to every individual the force and rights of humanhood?

Does your system guarantee absolute freedom of religion?

Is everyone in your community guaranteed food, shelter, protection, dignity, so long as your group has these things in its gift?

Does your system guarantee the tribal control of tribal interests?

Does your system guarantee to each man one vote; but so much influence as his character can command?

Does your system guarantee to each man the product of his industry?

Does your system accept the fact that material things are of doubtful or transient value, that the things of the spirit are all that are enduring and worthwhile?

Does your system set larger value on kindness than on rigorous justice?

Does your system discourage large material possessions in one man?

Does your system provide for the sick, the helpless, the weak, the old and the stranger?

Does your system guarantee the integrity of the natural group called the family?

Does your system recognize and further the fundamental thought that the chief duty of man is the attainment of manhood, which means the perfect and harmonious development of every part and power that goes to make a man; and the consecration of that manhood to the service of one's people?

By every one of these tests, the White Civilization is a failure.

How is it that we of the Whiteman's way have just as much food in the land as ever we had, just as much wealth as ever we had, just as much need for labor, just as much material of every kind, just as much readiness to work; and yet we are facing a breakdown because we cannot co-ordinate these things into effective action?

Our system has broken down—our Civilization is a failure. Wherever pushed to a logical conclusion, it makes one millionaire and a million paupers. There is no complete happiness under its blight.

Men of the White Race! We speak now as representative of the most heroic race the world has ever seen, the most physically perfect race the world has ever seen, the most spiritual Civilization the world has ever seen.

We offer you the Message of the American Indian, the Creed of Manhood. We advocate his culture as an improvement on our own, if perchance by belated repentance, remorse, restitution, and justification, we may save ourselves from Divine vengeance and total destruction, as did the Ninevites in their final stance; so that we may have a chance to begin again with a better, higher thought.

BIOGRAPHICAL NOTES

ERNEST THOMPSON SETON, co-founder of the Boy Scouts of America, naturalist, author, and painter, was born in England in 1860. His stories and paintings of wildlife are standard works on nature study and wood lore for boys and girls that continue to be used to this day. Together with Lord Baden-Powell, Seton created the Boy Scouts of America as an organization that respects nature's gifts. Seton, however, was especially concerned with the plight of the Native Americans as well as the environment, ideas which led to his founding of the Woodcraft League of America. Author of over 50 books, Seton's message that the natural world is to be respected and nurtured is more relevant today than ever before. Currently, the Ernest Thompson Seton Institute in Los Angeles, CA is dedicated to preserving Seton's art and writings.

JULIA M. SETON (nee Buttree) married Ernest Thompson Seton in El Paso, Texas in 1935. She was a student at Hunter College, New York, and an author who published extensively on Native American arts, crafts, and music. Her first book, *Rhythm of the Redman*, was illustrated by Seton, and was published before they married. Julia worked as Seton's assistant and they both gave lectures at schools, clubs, and churches throughout the United States, Canada, France, England, and the Czech Republic. After Seton's death in 1946, Julia continued to write and maintain the Santa Fe estate, and also lectured on her own. She suffered a stroke in 1968 and died in Santa Fe in 1975.

PAUL GOBLE'S many awards as an author and illustrator of children's books include the prestigious Caldecott Medal. A native of England, Goble studied at the Central School of Art in London, but has lived in the United States since 1977 and became a citizen in 1984. Goble's lifelong fascination with the Native Americans of the Plains began during his childhood when he became intrigued with their culture and spirituality. His illustrations accurately depict Native American clothing, customs, and surroundings in brilliant color and detail. Goble researches ancient stories and retells them for his young audience in a manner sympathetic to Native American life ways. To date he has illustrated over 28 books. He has given his collection of original illustrations to the South Dakota Art Museum in Brookings, South Dakota. He and his wife live in Rapid City, South Dakota.

DEE SETON BARBER is the adopted daughter of Ernest Thompson Seton and Julia M. Seton. She is an expert advisor to Seton scholars, collectors, and Woodcrafters worldwide, and was the custodian of Seton Castle in Santa Fe, New Mexico until it was recently sold in 2004. She currently resides in Bristol, Tennessee.

INDEX OF AMERICAN INDIAN NAMES

For a glossary of all key foreign words used in books published by
World Wisdom, including metaphysical terms in English, consult:
www.DictionaryofSpiritualTerms.com
This on-line Dictionary of Spiritual Terms provides extensive defini-
tions, examples, and related terms in other languages.

OTHER BOOKS BY
ERNEST THOMPSON SETON

During his life Ernest Thompson Seton was a prolific author. He wrote numerous books and articles, many of which have been re-printed in multiple editions. Below is a selected bibliography of some of Thompson Seton's works, arranged in chronological order by the year of their original publication.

Mammals of Manitoba	1886
Birds of Manitoba	1891
How to Catch Wolves	1894
Studies in the Art of Anatomy of Animals	1896
Wild Animals I Have Known	1898
The Trail of the Sandhill Stag	1899
Lobo, Rag, and Vixen	1899
The Biography of a Grizzly	1900
Lobo	1900
Ragylug	1900
Lives of the Hunted	1901
Krag and Johnny Bear	1902
How to Play Indian	1903
Two Little Savages	1903
How to Make a Real Indian Teepee	1903
How Boys Can Form a Band of Indians	1903
The Red Book	1904
Monarch, the Big Bear of Tallac	1904
Woodmyth and Fable	1905
Animal Heroes	1905
The Birchbark Roll of the Woodcraft Indians	1906
The Natural History of the Ten Commandments	1907
Fauna of Manitoba	1909
Biography of a Silver Fox	1909
Life-Histories of Northern Animals	1909
A Handbook of Woodcraft, Scouting, and Life-Craft, *Including General Sir Baden-Powell's Scouting for Boys*	1910
The Forester's Manual	1910

The Arctic Prairies	1911
Rolf in the Woods	1911
The Book of Woodcraft and Indian Lore	1912
Wild Animals at Home	1913
The Slum Cat	1915
Legend of the White Reindeer	1915
The Manual of the Woodcraft Indians	1915
Wild Animal Ways	1916
Woodcraft Manual for Girls	1916
The Preacher of Cedar Mountain	1917
Woodcraft Manual for Boys: The Sixteenth Birch Bark Roll	1917
Sign Talk of the Indians	1918
The Laws and Honors of the Little Lodge of Woodcraft	1919
The Brownie Wigwam: The Rules of the Brownies	1921
The Buffalo Wind	1921
Woodland Tales	1921
The Book of Woodcraft	1921
The Book of Woodcraft and Indian Lore	1922
Bannertail: The Story of a Gray Squirrel	1922
The Ten Commandments in the Animal World	1923
Animals	1926
Animals Worth Knowing	1928
Krag, the Kootenay Ram and Other Stories	1929
Billy the Dog that Made Good	1930
Cute Coyote and Other Stories	1930
Lobo, Bingo, the Pacing Mustang	1930
Famous Animal Stories	1932
The Gospel of the Redman (with Julia Seton)	1936
Biography of an Arctic Fox	1937
Great Historic Animals	1937
Mainly About Wolves	1937
Trail and Camp-Fire Stories	1940
Trail of an Artist-Naturalist: The Autobiography of Ernest Thompson Seton	1940
The Best of Ernest Thompson Seton	1949
Ernest Thompson Seton's America: Selections of the Writings of the Artist-Naturalist	1954
Animal Tracks and Hunter Signs	1958
The Worlds of Ernest Thompson Seton	1976

Titles in the Spiritual Classics Series by World Wisdom

The Buddha Eye:
An Anthology of the Kyoto School and Its Contemporaries,
edited by Frederick Franck, 2004

A Christian Women's Secret:
A Modern-Day Journey to God,
by Lilian Staveley, 2008

The Essential Writings of Charles Eastman (Ohiyesa),
edited by Michael Oren Fitzgerald, 2007

Gospel of the Redman,
compiled by Ernest Thompson Seton and
Julia M. Seton, 2005

Introduction to Sufi Doctrine,
by Titus Burckhardt, 2008

Lamp of Non-Dual Knowledge & Cream of Liberation:
Two Jewels of Indian Wisdom,
by Sri Swami Karapatra and Swami Tandavaraya,
translated by Swami Sri Ramanananda Saraswathi, 2003

Music of the Sky:
An Anthology of Spiritual Poetry,
edited by Patrick Laude and Barry McDonald, 2004

The Mystics of Islam, by Reynold A. Nicholson, 2002

Naturalness: A Classic of Shin Buddhism,
by Kenryo Kanamatsu, 2002

The Path of Muhammad:
A Book on Islamic Morals and Ethics,
by Imam Birgivi, interpreted by Shaykh Tosun Bayrak, 2005

Pray Without Ceasing:
The Way of the Invocation in World Religions,
edited by Patrick Laude, 2006

The Quiet Way: A Christian Path to Inner Peace,
by Gerhard Tersteegen,
translated by Emily Chisholm, 2008

Tripura Rahasya:
The Secret of the Supreme Goddess, translated by
Swami Sri Ramanananda Saraswathi, 2002

The Way and the Mountain:
Tibet, Buddhism, and Tradition,
by Marco Pallis, 2008